# Wings
# of Illusion

Dedicated to my wife Cheryl for her help, inspiration, and encouragement

# Wings
# of Illusion

The Origin,
Nature and Future of
Paranormal Belief

## JOHN F. SCHUMAKER

**Prometheus Books**

59 John Glenn Drive
Amherst, New York 14228-2197

Published 1990 by Prometheus Books

Inquiries should be addressed to
Prometheus Books
59 John Glenn Drive
Amherst, New York 14228–2197
VOICE: 716–691–0133, ext. 207
FAX: 716–564–2711
WWW.PROMETHEUSBOOKS.COM

Originally published in the U.K. by Polity Press in Association with Basil Blackwell

Library of Congress Card Catalog Number 90–61125

ISBN-13: 978–0–87975–624–6

ISBN-10: 0–87975–624–1

Printed in the United States of America on acid-free paper

# Contents

# Preface

The reader may look upon this as a strange book, and there are several reasons for this. One is that the human being is such a strange and mysterious creature. I have written here a book on the origin, nature, and function of our belief in the paranormal. That in itself is not so strange. There are many people like myself who find it intensely interesting that members of our species are able to believe the unbelievable. What is strange, however, is that much of the motivation for writing this book stems from a powerful urge to understand the destructive and seemingly suicidal qualities that are features of the human animal. Throughout the writing of this book, I continually reminded myself of a character in Thornton Wilder's *The Eighth Day* who is overwhelmed by the mad cruelty that human beings show to each other. He realizes the extent of our inhumanity to each other, and concludes that "the whole world's wrong," that there is something terribly flawed at the very heart of the human animal.[1] He then takes it upon himself to track down the problem.

In the pages to follow, I too attempt to track down that "problem," that "something wrong." I discover that it is the human appetite for illusion and self-deception which usually comes packaged as paranormal belief. If that isn't odd enough, I also show that this "problem" has always been a blessing and solution for us as well. I make the seemingly strange case that evolution saved us from an early prototype of intelligence by giving us the capacity to be suggestible and hypnotizable. At that point, all reality-transcending belief, including religion, was born.

In contrast to most books dealing with paranormal belief, I

point out that this particular human ability is taking us down the road to self-extinction. That "something wrong" is a flaw in what I call the "paranormal belief imperative." As a life-threatening flaw, it is probably part of what Carl Sagan called the "excess evolutionary baggage" that we are forced to carry around, despite its counterproductive effects on us in modern times.[2]

A good deal of evidence is offered to show that paranormal belief promotes personality characteristics that underlie small-scale and large-scale inhumanity. Very few people are without a certain degree of paranormal belief. Although most of us are not consciously aware of it, paranormal belief is our strongest drive. In the past, we were able to live with the destructiveness that goes hand in hand with our defiance of the natural order. Unfortunately, the nuclear age has changed all that. I describe the biological checkmate that we face as creatures who, in the past, had to become the stupidest as well as the brightest of all earthly inhabitants. I also discuss the interesting role that culture plays in prescribing and safeguarding certain agreed-upon forms of "stupidity."

Stranger than all that is the way that certain types of psychological disturbances are tied to our drive for self-deception. I step aside from my cheerless forebodings in order to describe new ways to understand and treat an entire class of mental illness. These "monoideistic" disorders are problems that we now realize are dysfunctions of the suggestibility process. I refer to them as "problems of religion." The one that I describe in greatest depth is anorexia nervosa. I believe a "religious" understanding of mental illness offers great promise for a re-working of the clumsy ways in which we now try to understand abnormal behavior. The reader will probably rebel at one stage and realize that it is a contradiction to concentrate on helping single members of a species when that entire species is about to self-destruct. My response is that this is a book about contradictions. It is about the only animal that *naturally* does things that do not make sense. Then again, there is hope in the possibility that I am wrong in everything I say. Even if I am right in viewing us as dinosaurs awaiting our turn for extinction, there is still the present. And despite the villain that I play here, I share the same desire of which Albert Camus spoke – to help reduce the sum total of human suffering and bitterness that poisons humankind. This book will probably not prevent the human being from continuing to "spin on its age-old demonic career," as Ernest Becker puts it in

*The Denial of Death.* But if I cannot help to reduce the bitterness that now poisons us, maybe I can do that little bit to alleviate the mental anguish that some of us must bear. There must be some merit to that, even if there is no ultimate meaning or sense to such endeavors.

The reader will see that I take the liberty of wearing a number of hats. I confess to getting annoyed at scholars who become so specialized that they end up looking at the world through miniscule pinholes. They lack the global perspective I value so much. Divergent thinking is a lost art. I recall an incident in my last year as an undergraduate at the University of Wisconsin, when I was working as a research assistant to the world's foremost authority on methods by which the eye-blink response can become conditioned. I sought his advice on which sub-area of psychology I should pursue in graduate school. He asked me whether I wanted to push grains of sand or whether I wanted to sink shafts. "Definitely sink shafts," I replied. All he could do was to steer me away from those branches of psychology that involved nothing but the pushing of sand grains. I went on to become a clinical psychologist. Over time, I came to realize that very few people in any branch of psychology are trying to sink theoretical shafts. They are focusing on details. They are *lost* in details. The years have confirmed that one forfeits creativity when one gets too close to the questions one asks.

This book is a bold attempt to sink what I feel is an important theoretical shaft. It has demanded a difficult rejection and unlearning of most of what I previously held to be true about the human being. It was also necessary to explore areas that are off-limits to a pinhole psychologist. At times, I don hats normally worn by evolutionary biologists, anthropologists, literary experts, theologians, culture theorists, philosophers, and troublemakers. Sand-pushers from any of these disciplines could easily accuse me of trespassing. They might even charge me with not knowing that certain grains of sand cannot be used to support my shaft. None the less, I am firmly convinced that new strides in self-understanding require us to draw liberally from all disciplines and every possible source of knowledge about ourselves. In building my case, I mention the work of many excellent sand-pushers. Still, I have used here a large canvas and a big brush. If some details have been smudged or neglected along the way, I can only hope that the final picture is big enough and clear enough still to be recognized as basically true.

The first mental blueprint for this book can be traced to a hot summer day in Hiroshima, Japan over ten years ago. I had been sickened by the displays and exhibits I had seen in the museum that stands on the site of the 1945 nuclear blast. Afterwards, I sat on a nearby parkbench, flooded with angry sadness. I searched every recess of my mind for the identity of that historical "something wrong" with our species. Around me was the irony that is the backbone of our species. I sat there expecting all of creation to cry with me, but the whole world seemed to be laughing. A group of uniformed schoolgirls ran up to me and asked if they could practise their English. They giggled joyfully between questions. "Where do you come from?" "Are houses *very* big in America?" "Have you been to Dallas?" They looked like a priceless collection of perfect porcelain dolls, each one more adorable than the other. In the background, I could see the twisted metal girders and shattered mortar of the only building to even partially withstand the nuclear horror that hit Hiroshima. It stood as it did that day in 1945. The contrast to the sweet children was infinite. When they had enough of me and marched off, I began to laugh inexplicably. But my laughter carried the heavy weight of the anguish that gnawed at me that day. Then some questions hounded me. There seemed an emotional urgency to them. "Why do we kill each other?" "Why does irrationality continue to haunt and terrorize a big-brained creature so capable of logic and reason?" "Can there be a future for evil angels that flit between such extremes of sense and nonsense?"

Since that unsettling day in Hiroshima, I have come to realize that this "something wrong" is the illusive beast of paranormal belief. It is our best friend and our most dreaded foe. It shows itself everywhere, and for that very reason, it is hard to see. It cannot be found by taking the usual roads to knowledge. It slips away like mercury when one tries to converge on it through pinholes. Pushing grains of sand is not enough. Instead, we must not be afraid to entertain illogic in trying to understand an animal with such an ambivalent relationship with logic. Seemingly parallel concepts must be allowed to intersect. Squares must fit into circular slots, and vice versa. It is necessary, as Rank once said, to let one's thoughts "spread ever outward until they break on the edge of the unthinkable."[3]

The beast we shall discover is certainly a strange one. It lives at that unthinkable edge. There, this beast is fed on the untruths that we hold to be true. Therefore, it is necessary to approach it with the motto of famous architect Frank Lloyd Wright: "Truth against the world!" To learn the truth about ourselves, we are pitted against the whole world of people, including ourselves. Our intellectual hunt ends as an empty victory. We find that we are prisoners of what it is we have been seeking. Many will deem it strange, as well as disappointing, that the deadly "something wrong" in us cannot be slain or even tamed. None the less, I hope the reader finds this a stimulating adventure.

I would like to thank Anthony Giddens for his enthusiasm concerning this venture, and for his useful comments which enabled me to carry my ideas to their logical conclusions.

# 1   *In Search of Ourselves*

We have tried so many times, and in so many ways, to understand ourselves. Each time, however, a credible model by which to make sense of our uniquely human behavior seems to elude us. As we get closer to self-understanding, it seems that "everything intercepts us from ourselves," as Emerson wrote in his 1883 work, *Journals*. In *Duino Elegies*, Rainer Maria Rilke compared us to dew on new grass since "what we are always rises away from us."[1]

In search for a true image of ourselves we have, at varying times, seen ourselves as gods, animals, and machines. We have occasionally conceived of ourselves as approaching the sublime, while at other times reduced ourselves to the mere personification of mindless and automatic drives and impulses. We have been everything and nothing, and all measures of all things in between those extremes. Yet always, as we reach out to grasp what we think the mirror reflects, the image shifts and we come away with still another conceptual model that somehow fails to explain us to ourselves.

As a psychologist, I have often wondered why my chosen profession had not made more obvious contributions to our embarrassingly small pool of knowledge about human behavior. Unfortunately, what we see is a once promising field of study that remains tangled in a barren wasteland of contrived and recycled theories about human thought, feeling, and action. This situation led Ernest Becker to say that modern psychology is suffering from a "general imbecility," a severe myopia that promotes intellectual paralysis and theoretical stagnation.[2] More and more people are agreeing with John Dewey's description of the field of psychology when he called it "a mass of cant, of slush, of superstition worthy of the most flourishing days of the medicine man."[3] Some might find such criticisms unduly harsh and unwarranted. The fact remains that the disconcerting numbers of inconsistent and mutually incompatible theories on any one topic are irritating, if not downright exasperating, to the dedicated student of the human condition.

Now, more than ever, we need to make new and innovative psychological inroads, which will enable us to determine finally the true identity of the human being. The world has become dangerously complex and filled with ever more challenging problems. Our technological knowledge has raced light years ahead of even a basic knowledge of the very creature responsible for the breathtaking scientific strides that reshape our world. Technical advances have us balanced precariously on the edge of self-extinction. We cannot afford to be in ignorance about ourselves at such a time. It is a time that holds not only increasing risks, but promises of unparalleled opportunity for the betterment of the human condition on a global level.

It has been pointed out that, whenever the ratio of what is known to what needs to be known approaches zero, we are inclined to concoct false "knowledge" and to pretend that we know more than we actually do. Although the ratio now stands near zero, we can no longer rely on pseudo-knowledge and a hatful of psycho-babble and psychologisms to get us by. As Robert Pirsig understood, psycho-babble and "pop" theories are worse than no knowledge at all, since they are often mistaken for the truth and only serve to retard an eventual understanding of ourselves.[4]

One reason we in psychology have been spinning our wheels is that we have been reluctant to abandon the familiar notion that we are principally "psychological" beings. Let me stick my neck out and say that we shall never understand ourselves from within the confines of the psychological sciences alone. As a framework within which to view ourselves, the psychological model of the human being is a myth. It fails to embrace other dimensions of the overall human makeup. We are far more than psychological creatures. This is exactly the reason why none of the existing schools of psychological thought comes remotely close to discovering the heart and inner workings of our fascinating species.

Some frustrated thinkers now hold that the riddle of human

behavior will never be solved. They claim that the human brain is inherently incapable of understanding itself. It has even been argued that our brains have evolved so as to prevent us from recognizing the cognitive ploys we employ in coping with the human condition.[5] Others have resolved the perplexing problem of discovering human nature by claiming that humanity is completely plastic, without a "nature" at all.[6] While new ways of approaching ourselves may be necessary, I do not believe the puzzle of human behavior is without an eventual solution. Also, I do not adhere to the prospect that we are without a fundamental nature that can be extracted from the diverse and often confusing behavior that we observe in ourselves.

Any sound formulation of our actual natures must account for the endless contradictions that characterize the human animal. Possibly more than anything else, we are contradictions. This alone confounds any theory that attempts to make sense of, or impose laws and logic on, human action and endeavor. Rilke captured the essence of our nature and destiny when he said we are meant "to be opposites, always, and nothing but opposites."[7] Pascal, in *Pensées*, highlighted this aspect of our nature when he wrote so beautifully:

> What a chimera then is man!
> How strange and monstrous!
> A chaos, a subject of contradictions,
>     a prodigy.
> Judge of all things, yet a stupid
>     earthworm;
> Depository of truth, yet a cesspool
>     of uncertainty and error;
> The glory and the refuse of the universe,
> Who will unravel this tangle?[8]

Physically, we may not resemble the mythological chimera, that fire-belching monster with a goat's body, a lion's head, and a serpent's tail. In all other respects, however, we have definite chimera-like qualities that reveal themselves in the entire spectrum of our behavior. We are unquestionably a creature of genius with awesome intellectual ability. At the same time, we are akin to an earthworm engaging in actions of such stupidity that our own survival is jeopardized. We stand alone in the animal kingdom with our highly specialized logic and reasoning that summon us toward new truths. Yet we turn around and show that we are cesspools of irrationality ready to defend and even die for something in total defiance of that same logic and reason. We are capable of remarkably sensitive, higher-order information-processing on the one hand, and of the most stumfumbling distortions of bold-faced facts on the other. We glorious creatures can be indescribably tender and kind, and risk our very lives for a single soul in distress. At another time or place, however, we are just as apt to play a part in equally unimaginable acts of savagery and total disregard for life.

We have become so totally accustomed to contradictions in ourselves that we no longer even see them as contradictions. Yet, none of the ways by which we try to understand ourselves can adequately account for our chimera-like features. If one imposes logic on our behavior, it really makes no sense that the creature that has come to control nature and the planet should create as much pain for itself as it alleviates. It makes no sense that the same animal that goes to such heartwarming lengths to eliminate suffering and give life to its own kind can simultaneously engage in the pitiless slaughter of endless thousands of its own kind. No present theoretical framework effectively combines and makes sense of the extremes of genius and stupidity, caring and brutality, nobility and degradation. We must find how these fuse together in our curious species.

All existing theories about ourselves are far too "sensible" and inclined to specify laws and rules that govern our actions. They, of course, can only describe small and isolated aspects of our overall makeup. None of the familiar modes of psychological thought has found the key that can unlock the mystery of human behavior in all its puzzling and self-confounding intricacies. The question has always been and remains the question about the true source of human motivation.

Psychoanalysts have searched in vain for the sexual basis of our actions. As some critics have said, what they have achieved is a cure that still searches for a disease. Behaviorists typically ignore innate determinants of behavior, while getting lost in the specifics of the learning process. Social learning theorists come closer to the mark, but they too have failed to recognize the fact that we have a biological nature that precedes learning. Many cognitive psychologists have resurrected the errant notion that we are fundamentally rational and that our conscious thought processes dictate our behavior. Cognitive behaviorists, who are currently in the ascendant, have forced an unworkable marriage between cognitive and behavioral theory. That unlikely combination offers little more theoretical promise than any of the others, as it does not take into account the single most powerful of all human drives. Humanists enter from the far left with an ill-defined theoretical stance that sees us as being pre-programmed to become ever more actualized, autonomous, and perfect. If ever something was *not* true, it is the proposition that the human animal is born to be good! In short, we simply cannot advance our knowledge of ourselves with any of our contemporary theoretical models as they now stand. And, with current therapies based on these formulations, it is no wonder that studies have surfaced showing randomly selected housewives and other untrained people to be better agents of change than professional therapists.

Defenders of our major systems of psychological thought spend endless hours arguing the relative merits of their largely opposed approaches. In fairness, it should be acknowledged that each of these formulations emphasizes important dimensions of ourselves. On the other hand, none of these systems has tapped the true source of human motivation. None has built a foundation for their theory on the real driving force behind our behaviour, namely the drive for illusion, self-deception, and reality distortion.

I want to show that we are, pre-eminently, auto-hypnotic creatures that must believe ourselves into reality shelters and states of psychic anesthesia. It will be seen that, although there are inferior alternatives, paranormal belief is the intended and easiest method by which this onerous task is accomplished. I will speak of the paranormal model of ourselves, rather than the psychological, sexual, or rational model. We must focus on the *paranormal belief imperative* rather than the array of other drives that are incorrectly thought to make us the unique creature that we are.

The paranormal belief motive is so obvious and all-pervasive that it is hard to see. It shows itself everywhere, which makes it as difficult to grasp as if it were to be seen nowhere at all. It is the canvas against which all other facets of human consciousness and human endeavor are painted. The extent to which this motive is satisfied is an important factor determining our general functioning ability and overall mental health.

Evidence that we are creatures of the paranormal can be found when we look at behavior *across* the many different cultures of the world. The reason we do this is twofold. First, it tells us if a certain type of behavior is universal or if it emerges only under certain cultural conditions; and second, a cross-cultural analysis can give us a good idea of the degree to which something is learned, as compared to being fixed to our biological or genetic endowments. As a rule, the closer a behavior is to being universal in nature, the more inclined we are to think that such a behavior is crucial to survival. We even suspect that such behaviors may have a physiological basis. We look differently upon behaviors that appear in some cultures but not in others. In such cases, we assume a large learning or conditioning component and are less likely to view that form of behavior as crucial for survival. This is especially true if a behavioral pattern that appears in one or more cultures is nonexistent in others. Romantic love is an example of this latter case. It abounds and flourishes in most Western societies, and this could lead one to assume that it is common to all human societies. When one looks at the phenomenon cross-culturally, however, it becomes apparent that romantic love is generally limited to Western societies and is frequently completely absent from groups in non-Western cultures.

When we apply the cross-cultural litmus-test to the entire range of human behavior, we find something very interesting. We see that only *one* category of behavior is universal by the strictest definition. That is paranormal believing. Cultural anthropologists and cross-cultural psychologists have yet to isolate a single society in which its people do not have longstanding and well-developed systems of paranormal belief. Although some other human traits are common to most cultures, none is as widespread and pervasive as beliefs that transcend reality and the normal order of earthly events.

Sexual motivation does not even survive as a universal constant when placed under close cross-cultural scrutiny. Of course, all peoples of the world rely upon sexual activities for reproductive purposes. Beyond that, we tend to impose the "pressure cooker" idea to what we call our sexual "appetites." We are usually led to believe that we can go without sex for a while, but that sexual tension will build and build if we remain celibate for too long. Carried to its logical conclusion, this view would have us frothing like rabid dogs and ready to erupt if denied a sexual outlet for extended periods. Certainly, the well-known "self-fulfilling prophecy" makes some of us foam a bit at the mouth. That is, we feel and act as if sexually deprived because we think sufficient time has transpired that we should be experiencing sexual deprivation.

That is a product of our cultural conditioning, for the sexual imperative is a myth.

There are many people in our own society who survive perfectly well without sexual activity. When they claim to be relatively untroubled by their celibacy, we do not believe them. We think they are so far removed from their feelings that they would not know a sexual urge from a toothache. Or we surmise that some deeply embedded unconscious conflict has compelled them to repress their feelings and to live in the safety of asexuality. Their scenario gathers credence when we realize that entire societies exist in which sexual activity is seen as anything but a necessarily frequent activity. The Grand Valley Dani people of New Guinea, for example, customarily abstain from sexual intercourse for up to six years following the birth of a child. They resort to no alternative sexual outlets, and report no build-up of tension or sexual frustration. Anthropologists have found no ill-effects from this culturally-based practice.[9] Numerous other cultures appear to have remarkably low levels of sexual motivation and to have no concept resembling our "pressure cooker" view of sexuality. Their lids do not blow off for the simple reason that sex is not our primary motive. We can carry on without sex.

From a global perspective, we can see that we are able to live with – or without – almost anything. We can adjust to and accommodate almost any physical, social, or cultural conditions. In that sense, we are *almost* indefinitely malleable. The only exception is that we do not seem able to live without belief, and in particular belief in something, someone, or some force that simplifies and/or supersedes the reality of the human situation. Less than one percent of people, *regardless of culture*, have no paranormal beliefs at all. The same invariance cannot be seen in any other form of human behavior.

Eugene Kennedy, in his excellent work on the dynamics of belief, states that the human being is fundamentally "a believing phenomenon who must believe in order to live at all."[10] He astutely notes that belief is as indispensable to us as air and water. Without it, he adds, we fall victim to personality disintegration and a preponderance of negative repercussions to our psychological well-being. Kennedy also observes the near impossibility of escaping from these reality-defying beliefs. This is equally true of the people who, superficially, seem to be unbelievers. In order to achieve and maintain an optimal level of emotional and psychological intactness, we must defeat objective reality. The intended weapon is paranormal belief in all its splendid colors and potential variations.

Before proceeding with a detailed description of our need and ability to conquer reality, let me clarify the way in which I employ the word "reality." Psychologists are sometimes criticized for the loose and intemperate use of "reality." It undeniably holds an esteemed place in the professional nomenclature of many psychologists, most notably clinical psychologists. They have even been known to advise that certain people be placed in institutions for being "out of touch" with their conception of "reality." However, I use that word in a very different sense in this book. Here, it will refer to the harsh and inescapable aspects of the human condition, especially those that could force us to take refuge in beliefs based outside the natural order of earthly events. This is a common usage of the term and the one intended by several other thinkers to whom I shall refer on this subject.

Death and our awareness of our personal mortality represent one dimension of reality, as the word is used in this context. Ernest Becker, in his Pulitzer prize-winning classic *The Denial of Death*, wrote that "a full apprehension of man's condition would drive him insane."[11] He argues that our unique ability to perceive and understand death impels us to invent paranormal "lies" about reality. These cushion us from the otherwise paralyzing *reality* of impending death.

Becker's untimely death was a great loss to all serious students of the human condition. He was gifted with what one reviewer of his work called "electrifying intelligence." As one of the greatest thinkers of the twentieth century, I believe his works will continue to grow in popularity as the rest of the world catches up with his revolutionary ideas. The discovery of Becker's work, more than anything else, allowed my ideas about the innermost workings of the human being to fall into place; and his ideas form part of the backdrop for some of the arguments I present in this book. The same is true for other thinkers who had a significant influence on Becker. These include Soren Kierkegaard, Henri Bergson, Otto Rank, and Arthur Koestler. It seems fitting that Becker's primary inspiration, Otto Rank, was also the author of the book, *Art and Artist*, which I read as a teenager and which made me decide to take up psychology. Although some of my own ideas do not align with their views, I find it sad that existential pathfinders like Becker and Rank are rarely included in the curricula of present-day courses of study. The innovative work of Mordecai Kaffman was also helpful in giving final shape to my views. In addition, I draw upon certain thoughts and ideas that are contained in works of fiction. We in psychology tend to be afraid to express an idea that is not measured and chopped into a thousand disparate pieces. Authors like Saul Bellow and Thornton Wilder, as only two examples, have the ability to give penetrating insights into human behavior without that same self-consciousness and self-inhibition.

By his own admission, Becker was not a clinical psychologist. In fact, his background was cultural anthropology. None the less, he tried to translate his brilliant ideas into a new explanation of mental illness. Becker justified his effort by saying that, in such a stagnant and stifling period in psychological thought, someone had to play the fool and start somewhere in combating our intellectual myopia. Noting how we have gravitated toward cumbersome and misguided theories on our recent dead-end theoretical runs, he also made the case that "today we need simple-mindedness in order to be able to say anything at all."[12] If there is a weakness in Becker's work, I feel it lies in his attempt to reformulate contemporary views on mental illness. As a clinical psychologist, I feel in a somewhat more advantaged position in trying to undertake such a reformulation. Additionally, I have spent the past several years conducting research that can provide quantitative support for some of the concepts underlying these new views on mental illness as well as mental health. Furthermore, I attest to being simple-minded enough to make this re-approach straightforward and accessible to a broad spectrum of the general population. Being foolish as well, I shall rely on the insight of William Blake who wrote, in *Proverbs of Hell*, that fools who persist in their folly will eventually become wise.

I shall only use Becker and the above-mentioned thinkers as a springboard for the further development of the sketchy view of ourselves as inhabitants of the paranormal. I shall also take this opportunity to put the fascinating phenomena of suggestibility, waking hypnosis, and the paranormal belief imperative into evolutionary perspective. I wholeheartedly agree with Stephen Jay Gould who wrote in *Ever since Darwin* that "the evolutionary perspective is the antidote to our cosmic arrogance."[13] Also, the position will be taken that death represents just one dimension of the "reality" from which we must find psychic sanctuary. As we shall see in chapter 2, the evolution of consciousness required that we find a means to defend our emotional world from the perception of other potentially debilitating realities. It will be shown that paranormal belief prevented the extinction of our species, the one whose survival depended on a highly dangerous form of intelligence. A chapter is also devoted to weighing up the relative benefits and costs of both religious and non-religious paranormal belief, including a summary of research into the effects that belief and unbelief have on personality and mental health. Next, I isolate some specific forms of mental illness that have previously eluded our understanding. These include anorexia nervosa, obsessions, compulsions, paranoia, and other "mono-ideistic" disorders, which can be explained as "problems of religion." The last chapter of this volume focuses on the real possibility that our species has reached an evolutionary impasse. Since paranormal belief has destructiveness toward both self and others as one costly consequence, we shall ask if there are other ways to cope with the unnerving realities of the human condition.

A few words of preparation are in order before we proceed. First, no real distinction will be made between religious and non-religious paranormal beliefs. A number of authors have recognized that they do not differ significantly in their general manner of expression or their separation of concepts such as body, soul, and mind. Religious and non-religious paranormal belief systems are similar in their implicit assertion that our reality is not the only or the true one.[14] Therefore, some religious toes are bound to be stepped on as these beliefs are grouped together with the myriad of other paranormal reality shelters. The topic of religion is so charged emotionally that few psychologists have dared to venture into a scientific study of this aspect of human behavior. Yet, many large pockets of ignorance remain concerning our knowledge of ourselves, and I feel a bold objective analysis of religious belief and behavior could fill some of these.

An appreciation of the ideas presented here also requires that we question some of the basic assumptions we hold about ourselves and our place in nature. More courage than intelligence is required fully to understand ourselves. We must first strip away the many layers of cultural conditioning that represent so many intellectual and emotional security blankets. As we shall see later, culture is the purveyor of paranormal self-deceptions with which we cope with an otherwise terrifying world. It safeguards the beliefs of its members and provides unpleasant emotional consequences for those who do not utilize culture's paranormal offerings in re-shaping reality. To pull oneself out of the culturally conditioned schematics with which we perceive the world is no easy task. Unless we do so, however, we cannot fashion an image of ourselves in our own likeness.

One of the biggest intellectual blunders we make is when we operate from the assumption that we are more than, or fundamentally different from, other animals. That self-blinding premise, more than any other, has kept us orphans to ourselves, captives of our own intense drive to modify and reconstruct our perceptions of the world. It is a basic tenet of Christianity and one that many would find almost impossible to question seriously. A disconcerting question arises from a debate about the heritage of our curious species. Is our rightful home outside the earthly animal kingdom? An affirmative answer implies that we are more than the sum of our parts. From that starting point, there has come only a long series of self-aggrandizing theoretical monstrosities. These have only taken us further away from potential self-knowledge. That approach always becomes mired in a myriad of hypothetical constructs, which foster circular debates and lead us toward additional fictions about our essential natures. I have placed our paranormal belief imperative, as well as all behaviors deriving from this drive, in an evolutionary context. In this respect, I again agree with Gould who says that "our uniqueness arises from the operation of ordinary evolutionary processes, not from any predisposition toward higher things."[15] We do have dignity *within* nature. As we shall also see, human indignity and inhumanity are a direct consequence of striving to transcend nature and the normal.

Another debate that rages within psychology is the extent to which the human being is motivated by rational, in contrast to irrational, forces. The heat from this debate is generated by the false assumption that we must be one or the other. I want to show that, by our very nature, we are both rational and irrational creatures. Even more, it is our unique evolutionary task to find a point of harmony between the highly rational and highly irrational parts of us. We, in psychology, have been unable to reconcile the rational and irrational forces that determine the seemingly cryptic directions taken by human behavior.

Otto Rank saw through the myth that we operate according to "psychological" principles. He understood that we are essentially "theological" creatures whose primary quest and need is for life-enhancing illusion that can vanquish reality and its unsettling forebodings. The anthropologist Melford Spiro, whose ideas will be discussed shortly, also realized that "religion" is the most powerful of all human motivations. At the point of realization of our basically theological nature, psychology must give way to religion. It has little chance of advancing beyond its present infancy if it does not merge with the study of our strong "religious" leanings. This work involves a necessary blending of these two disciplines, while defining religion in the broadest possible way. As we explore the limits and implications for our impelling drive for illusion, I shall let psychology and religion merge and overlap as they claim their rightful positions. Religion, though, will be contained in a human frame of reference and treated as a necessary evolutionary strategy.

It would be arrogant to state unequivocally that we are not the children of one of the 2,000 or so gods that exist in the minds of the various peoples of the world. Also, it would be presumptuous to claim that I *know* we are only animals and that we are not the one special creature which should be singled out for study as somehow *more* than an animal. What I do know, however, is that the pieces of the human puzzle finally come together beautifully when we understand ourselves as animals that have evolved a mechanism by which to cope with our primary source of natural selection – intelligence. Of course, the paranormal escape from intelligence may make us feel like "spiritual" beings. This inevitably inclines us to impose more and more needless intangibles and hypotheticals on our theoretical formulas.

In his delightful *Devil's Dictionary*, Ambrose Bierce describes human existence as a "spiritual pickle preserving the body from decay."[16] He was justified in calling life a spiritual pickle because it *feels* spiritual. But I am convinced that it is no more than that – a feeling. And one that clouds our visions of ourselves. It leads us to inevitably conclude we are different from the rest of creation. In actuality, the road to self-understanding will only come into sight if we can resist the urge to elevate and spiritualize ourselves. This must be done while still recognizing that our one universal characteristic is to deny and/or reinterpret our world.

When we do this, the many opposites and contradictions that previously thwarted us begin to make sense. They, in fact, become the very clues we need to find our way through the jumble of misconceptions and disarrayed notions that have taken us so far from an honest picture of ourselves. We shall see how paranormal self-deception, as a necessary evolutionary adaptation, produces a chimera-like creature with opposing intellectual and behavioral dictates. What, on the surface, appear to be hopelessly incomprehensible contradictions are only displays of the fascinating psychic juggle performed by evolution's riskiest experiment. We, the children of the paranormal, are that experiment.

We are not about to embark on a reductionistic journey into despair. I also hope that we are not going to come away from this synthesis of ideas feeling less worthwhile or dignified. It is true that I shall depict some of our carefully nurtured beliefs, including religious ones, as coping mechanisms. It is also the case that this treatise places us squarely in the context of the animal kingdom and understands even our cherished "spiritual" natures according to an animal model. Admittedly, we may feel a little foolish when we let ourselves learn how the evolutionary hat-trick of paranormal belief works. On the other hand, I want to emphasize the potential promise that such a bold re-conceptualization holds. We now stand at the crossroads between self-extinction and a radically new maturity, which could conceivably save us from ourselves. We may very well choose the road to oblivion. Even so, we shall see that important benefits can be derived, which will assist us at this present time of unparalleled social and psychological ills.

# 2  *The Birth of the Paranormal*

Those who specialize in the study of evolution no longer refer to evolutionary principles as "theory." There is a point of certainty on any topic beyond which a theory becomes accepted as fundamentally true. Then, instead of squabbling about the true or false nature of the basic concept, the scientist can get on with the business of probing the depths and minute particulars of the fully accepted proposition. This is the case with evolution. Its veracity is not doubted by anyone who has made a serious inquiry into the subject. The evidence is monumental in proportion and unequivocal in nature. Like it or not, life as we know it *evolved*.

The essential elements of the evolutionary process are quite simple to understand. It is possible to isolate at least one primary basis for natural selection in every creature. In each case, it is an ability or characteristic that enables the organism to compete successfully for the ingredients of survival. Of course, the source of all those ingredients is the sun, without which no life in any form would exist on our planet. Survival entails the effective taking of life, the only exceptions being creatures that take *potential* life, such as seeds. This "nightmare spectacular" that has all earthly creatures soaking in each other's blood, as Becker describes it, is nothing but nature and natural selection in progress. As soon as a species becomes ill-equipped to secure an ample share of the fruits of the sun, it must adapt or become extinct. Contrary to what many think, extinction is a very natural process. In fact, the vast majority of all life-forms are now extinct.

It is nothing new. Most creatures become extinct for reasons connected with a failure to adapt as needed. Adapt sufficiently or perish – that is the simple rule which determines the fate of any species.

What is not so simple is to move from a study of physical evolution into the realm of *mental* processes that have emerged over the course of our evolutionary histories. It is one thing to chronicle the observable bodily changes that have taken place in the cause of survival. More challenging, however, is to ferret out the evolutionary development of brain abilities. One does not have the luxury of fossil remains and other tangible signs of "proof" for the adaptations in question. Still, there is no reason to suspect that mental or cognitive adaptations were not a vital feature in the development of our species. Considering that the brain became our source of natural selection, one could argue effectively that evolutionary workings involving our mental faculties were of primary importance.

What we have become, both physically and psychologically, was for a purpose. That purpose again was survival. It was no accident that we became a creature of apparent opposites. Coincidence was not responsible for our unique ability to combine genius-like yearnings for truth with a seemingly mindless willingness to accept the wholly unbelievable as fact. The delicate balance we maintain between truth and fiction is the hallmark of our species. One should not be too quick to dismiss our appetite for illusion as a mere idiosyncrasy of our species. We should also pause before jumping to the conclusion that we are "spiritual" beings that cannot be understood in an evolutionary context. Our unique species represents the end-product of an evolutionary "miracle" which endowed our species with the ability to deceive itself and to fashion a hybrid reality for itself.

Evolutionary biologists sometimes argue about what was the biggest and most noteworthy evolutionary move that took place in our primordial past. Some focus on physical changes in the hand which increased dexterity and maximized tool-making capabilities. Others concentrate on the transition to an erectile posture. Still others credit the female switch from the "heat" sexual pattern to the modern estrus cycle, characterized by continual sexual receptiveness. This adaptation is thought to be responsible for one-to-one bonding and the eventual evolution of the family and patterns of social cooperation as we know them today. A great many works have been written on these aspects of our evolution and are outside the scope of the present discussion.

I want to concentrate on the specific brain adaptation that led to the paranormal belief imperative. It is my opinion that this evolutionary stroke of genius stands out from all the others in its importance and far-reaching consequences. Its great significance is underscored by its being the riskiest evolutionary action ever taken by our species. As we shall see, the paranormal belief adaptation has become dangerous and now stands to undo us completely. If it does not work, we shall join the vast number of species which have, for their own reasons, become extinct. The gamble may have been necessary. It is probable that we reached a crisis-point in our history, when the unchecked big brain was threatening to work *too well* for its own good. Let us look more closely at the pros and cons of intelligence as an evolutionary adaptation.

## The collision of amplified consciousness and reality

It is a basic law of evolution that creatures adapt only when they need to adapt; that is, when it increases their likelihood of survival. Often environmental changes force adaptation. We have had to make far more adaptations than most animal species and these adaptations have not been limited to strictly physical alterations. The shark, for example, was one of nature's masterstrokes. It was so perfectly suited for survival that it has gone virtually unchanged for over one hundred million years. We have quite the reverse story, with many adaptations demanded in a very short space of evolutionary time. Some of these were physical changes that allowed our earliest ancestors to cope with new climatic conditions that forced us from the trees somewhere between 5 and 15 million years ago. Others, however, can be traced to the nature of consciousness itself and how we had to cope with the pitfalls of that burgeoning dimension of ourselves. We had to adapt to our own adaptations and none more than that of the big brain.

One could quickly exhaust oneself trying to define what is meant by the term "consciousness." It has been the source of intellectual discourse for all of recorded history. Consciousness *per se* is not what separates and differentiates us from the rest of the animal kingdom. We need to be more specific in our use of the word consciousness before we can determine how our mental processes differ from other animals. R. E. Passingham makes a delightfully entertaining attempt to isolate the cognitive changes that a chimpanzee would have to make in order to become human. [1] In so doing, he speaks of a number of ways in which the word consciousness can be used. He offers evidence to show that many animals along the phylogenetic scale (the scale from "primitive" to "complex" life-forms) deserve to be deemed conscious, regardless of the term's usage. For example, consciousness is sometimes used to refer to self-awareness or the ability to possess a self-identity. Many people cite this type of consciousness as the one that distinguishes our species from all others. However, research shows that chimpanzees are self-aware and that they possess a sense of self. This can be seen in studies which found that chimpanzees react to a mirror-image of themselves differently from the way they would react to another of their kind. Consciousness sometimes refers to an animal's capacity for conscious perception and a sense that it *knows what it is doing.* Again, however, a good deal of research suggests that we do not differ from many other animals in the sense that we can perceive and respond to our own behavior in the context of our environment. Other animals "know." The one way to qualify this might be to say that other animals do not know that they know. That is a crucial difference between us and the rest of the animal kingdom.

Passingham admits to a large mental gulf that separates us from our fellow creatures. This is created not so much by the presence of self-awareness and perceptual abilities as by the *degree* to which these have developed in our species. We seemed to have crossed what he called a "cerebral Rubicon." (The Rubicon was the river that limited Caesar's province and, once crossed, committed him to battle with Pompey.) There could be no safe retreat. So we probably traversed a developmental *threshold* that resulted in an unparalleled *degree* of self-awareness. Once we reached and passed that point of critical brain mass, all sorts of uniquely human behaviors became possible. One of these was language which further amplified the levels of intelligence that were attainable. We became able to process information in a radically new code, one which paved the way for hypothetical and abstract thinking, as well as anticipatory thought. Of course, the other side of the coin was that, once over the "cerebral Rubicon," there was no turning back intellectually. We were on a cognitive collision course with what we could then perceive with our amplified intelligence. We became prey to the truth about our very existence. We reached an evolutionary milestone which did not allow us to retreat to a more simple and peaceful level of awareness. We were also to fall from a state of "grace" in so far as we would lose forever the innocence of animals that do not set out maliciously to destroy their own kind. Our survival became dependent on the maintaining of these dizzying intellectual heights, yet those same heights had profound emotional ramifications for our species. Once on the other side of the intellectual Rubicon, we entered the realm of the paranormal. We were then forced to arm ourselves with irrationality and belief.

In a recent publication, I wrote that extreme intelligence, as the source of natural selection in our species, was not wholly adaptive.[2] By that I was specifying the potential emotional damage that can stem from the type of awareness emanating from our unusually great intellectual capacities. The ideal evolutionary scheme for us would have been to have the advantages of the big brain without the destructive emotional repercussions brought on by such heightened self-awareness. However, useful evolutionary adaptations are frequently a give-and-take proposition, with the advantages of the new benefits outweighing the new liabilities. In all probability, self-consciousness was one of the more unfortunate liabilities that accompanied the spectacular advantages of intelligence. If we personify evolution for a moment, however, we can safely say that self-consciousness was not evolution's desired goal. It wanted intelligence. Despite any incidental benefits that may have accompanied self-awareness, that faculty caused many problems requiring additional adaptations. The complex relationship between intelligence, self-consciousness, reality, and paranormal belief becomes clear when we look more closely at intelligence as a source of natural selection.

Experts on the subject of evolution believe that climatic changes made it no longer possible for our prehuman ancestors to survive as tree-dwellers. Those environmental changes meant that food was now on the ground. It also meant that the adaptation to tree-dwelling survival had become obsolete. Some of our early forebears were to successfully traverse the difficult evolutionary road to ground-level food gathering. Many authorities believe these were those who were able to make best use of their hands in locating and carrying food to safe venues. That may sound insignificant, but it may be exactly what made the brain become the source of natural selection for our species. This was because hand facility and "intelligence" were closely correlated. On one level, it was manual dexterity which was becoming the basis for survival. But what was really becoming the focus of natural selection was brain capacity. Those who made the necessary adaptation were the most intelligent of these creatures, the ones who went on to spread their intelligent genes.

Once intelligence was established as the basis for our survival, it would, like all adaptations, attempt to improve on itself. All adaptations continue until the new ability reaches its optimal form. This latter point is an important one, as it implies that evolution "knows" when an adaptation has been taken *far enough*. Evolution "knew," for example, that the giraffe's neck should not continue to get forever longer over time. If it had, the giraffe's neck would be several miles long by now and the poor beasts would have an impossible time reaching down to the trees. More likely, a giraffe species with necks too long for their environment would have joined the long list of other failed species. In order that we did not become extinct at the hands of what was also our key to survival, intelligence had to be checked and moderated as well.

Very few thinkers have made the association between an evolutionary attempt to regulate the effects of intelligence and the dawn of paranormal belief. The best summary of the birth of paranormal belief can be found in Henri Bergson's *The Two Sources of Morality and Religion*.[3] In particular, his work on this issue is to be found in his discussion of what he calls "static" as compared to "dynamic" religious paranormal beliefs. I believe that this theoretical formulation provides the best model for an understanding of the development and maintenance of all paranormal belief. Bergson acknowledges the many advantages provided by intelligence as the source of natural selection in our earliest battles for survival. Its evident purpose was to favor tool-making ability which enabled provision of food and shelter in that difficult period of environmental change. However, as the brain was expanding in capacity and functioning potential, a concomitant problem was developing. For what was undoubtedly the first occurrence of its kind since the beginning of life on earth, an animal was coming to conscious grips with reality. This new creature was also seeing how it was fitting into the conditions of this reality.

The problem with reality, then and now, is that it makes no sense. Things that affect us directly and, at the same time, make no sense are very frightening. Ernest Becker was probably right when he commented that terror is the *normal* emotional state for someone in full view and bearing the full psychic brunt of reality. Other writers have also concluded that the ability to perceive the *real* world, and our position in it, in an undistorted manner is not entirely desirable. T. S. Eliot writes in *Four Quartets* that "human kind cannot bear very much reality." Phillip Rieff implies the same when he says "the more deeply we see, the less healthy we are."[4] And when Sartre notes that the human being "thrives on blindness," he is referring to the inherent hazards of consciousness and self-awareness. In his existentialistic fervor, he called human existence a "useless passion" since we inevitably cope with consciousness by thoroughly deluding ourselves about the nature of the human condition. I would agree that our drive for blindness is a passionate one. But I would again maintain that this feature of our makeup is highly purposeful when examined in a historical context.

Bergson writes that human intelligence began as "pure intelligence." This is the type of intelligence that operates empirically or, in other words, solely on the basis of direct experience with incoming facts and information. Behavioral and experimental psychologists pride themselves on how they limit their interpretation of events and behavior in accordance with this method. It does not permit hypotheticals or any other intangible mental construct to be introduced into the understanding process. With "pure" intelligence, no deductions or conclusions would be possible if evidence were not directly forthcoming to justify them. Pure intelligence would only allow one to believe what was genuinely *believable* according to the facts at hand. If someone saw another person keel over and remain there motionless until the body decomposed and turned to dust, then that would be exactly what happened. In the mind of the person with only pure intelligence, that vanished body could not exist in the Happy Hunting Ground, or Nirvana, or Heaven, or anywhere else. Pure intelligence would not have allowed for Zeus, Santa Claus, or the soul. Events could only have made as much sense as the facts would have allowed. At that point in our past, evolution had not yet made it possible for us to believe the *unbelievable*. We also had no emotional insulation from the facts heralded by brute reality. Our "purely" intelligent ancestors had not yet defeated reality. They had not demolished it and reassembled it into a meeker and more orderly sort of ogre.

In *The Two Sources of Morality and Religion*, Bergson states that "pure" intelligence would have resulted in a degree of awareness so great as to *neutralize* the advantages made possible by the expanding cognitive powers. The sympathetic division of our nervous systems would have been in the "alarm" mode continually. A collective nervous breakdown would have transpired as our species collapsed under the weight of what Rank termed "too much reality." Pure intelligence as such would not have worked as the basis for natural selection. This would have been due to the harmful emotional fallout caused by overexposure to terrifying aspects of the reality coming into our newly expanded visions. As Becker observes, reality and fear go hand in hand. He adds that a "hyperanxious" animal would be the consequence of too much intellectual and emotional contact with the inexplicable and frequently horrific elements of our true condition.

Becker singles out death perception as by far the worst psychological backlash created by our becoming a self-aware creature. Becker regarded the evolutionary idea of a self-conscious animal as "ludicrous, if not monstrous," since it meant we could know that we were "food for worms."[5] The psychological bind in which our new aptitude to envision reality placed us can be seen in his statement: "Man is literally split in two: he has an awareness of his own splendid uniqueness in that he sticks out of nature with a towering majesty, and yet he goes back into the ground a few feet in order blindly and dumbly to rot and disappear forever."[6] He claims that evolution made an "unintended" mistake when it created an animal with an extensively developed associative cortex, one with the means to symbolize, bind time, and impede the immediacy of experience.[7]

Becker says that less cerebral forms of animal life escape having to live with this absurd but terrifying dilemma. They are fortunate in that they lack a "symbolic identity." This point is reiterated by J. Crook in his work *The Evolution of Human Consciousness*. He also maintained that fear of death "is clearly anchored . . . to the construct of self as an identity."[8] According to Crook, self-awareness and death awareness are opposite sides of the same coin, since the death of body implies an end to personal experience. He asserted that some sort of adaptation was necessary so we are not "ever wriggling on that hook of death awareness." The evolutionary biologist, Theodosius Dobzhansky, writes that "self-awareness and death awareness are probably *causally* related and appeared together in evolution."[9] By which, he means quite simply that our ability to comprehend death was a direct result of our enhanced comprehension of ourselves. While acknowledging the obvious evolutionary advantages of self-awareness, Dobzhansky sees no possible adaptive benefits from death awareness. He too regarded our new ability to *know* about the reality of death to be an unfortunate by-product of the brain's evolutionary development.

In his outstanding book *The Tangled Wing*, Melvin Konner expounds on the many ways that our emotional and intellectual wings have become entangled by our biologies. This includes the biology of our big brain which can psychologically enmesh us with grief when it takes us over the threshold of death perception. He writes about what are really unhappy birthdays:

> Each birthday a little death, each *rite de passage* another passage toward it. There is a sense in which life consists of a continual condition of grief and bereavement, during which we mourn the loss of ourselves. Think of the anger; think of the shock; think of the sadness . . . Is it any wonder that the world's religions, great and small, with their venerable mutually contradictory fictions and their insatiable taste for holy war, have such a grip on so many excellent minds? . . . At least they offer balm in the face of great pain.[10]

Few would argue that many positive ramifications could lead from the knowledge that personal consciousness will terminate and that our bodies will decompose. To reflect deeply on that prospect is to see the likelihood, not only of death itself, but the usual suffering and pain that accompany the death process. Additionally, there is the realization that this same annihilation process will engulf our loved ones. Beyond that are the questions that remain unanswered as one is catapulted into the conceptual void of mortality. With enlarged brain capacity came the potential to anticipate, and with that the dubious talent to imagine the absolute nothingness that must follow death. Samuel Beckett shows his respect for this void when he writes that "nothing is more real than nothing." Becker agrees and says that, without much-needed defense mechanisms in place, untempered death perception would bring about total psychic paralysis.

Although none has been as eloquent as Becker on the subject, a number of others have stated that death awareness can be debilitating to the individual. Zilboorg, for example, wrote that unmitigated consciousness of death would make one unable to function normally, and that this product of consciousness must be "properly repressed to keep us living with any modicum of comfort."[11] That is, we would be rendered incapable of the routine activities that would ensure the welfare of ourselves and our species generally. Zilboorg explained that many people believe that they are not fearful of their own mortality, but that this is only because that particular reality has been erased from the readily accessible reaches of everyday consciousness. It is the pre-eminent life-force and the universal self-preservation instinct that come up against the realization of awaiting disintegration. William James wrote lyrically about the "healthy-mindedness" in us that helps us ignore and forget the reality of death. He described its presence as making up the "evil background" of human consciousness.[12] In *Mr. Sammler's Planet*, Saul Bellow remarks how strangely we play with death. We do so, he says, because "humankind could not endure futurelessness." Peter Berger also saw the psychological and emotional complications that derive from the awareness of death. Without some method of moderating the impact of death perception, he contended, we would be racked with all-pervasive anxiety and "naked terror" so that "everyday life would be impossible."[13]

Reality became *too real* when it made its debut in the minds of the humanoids under discussion here. Death awareness and all its anxiety-generating implications contributed to the all-too-real nature of the human condition. Still, the problems presented by "pure intelligence" to our early evolutionary pioneers went far beyond that morbid component of reality. Reality is far more than death. It is nothing short of chaos.

José Ortega y Gasset describes the broader problem and reveals that death is only one of many apparently senseless brushstrokes that would amount to a picture of life as incomprehensible, causally disconnected, and generally disarrayed. He states that the lucid person is destined to see life as chaos in which he/she is lost, and where everything is problematic in the deepest sense of the word.[14] Berger also speaks of the "nightmare threats" of chaos that would lead the non-deluded mind to the unsavory hypothesis that life lacks all order and meaning.[15] Charles Case expounds on some of the encountered realities of our condition that would spell chaos to a creature unfortunate enough to be cursed with pure intelligence. Chaos is many things, it is "children being born while others die, or illness that comes for no reason, or lightning that strikes one and not another."[16] It also includes befuddling body sensations such as thirst, hunger, and various other urges and motivations. On top of these and most other aspects of reality that would have made no sense to the "pure" intellect, they all happen at once. Without some way to contain this perceptual mess, Case claims that "human behavior would have been chaotic and based primarily on direct innate responses to stimuli."[17] He reasons that it is unlikely we would have survived as a species under such circumstances.

What is even worse is that an undistorted view of reality would reveal the panic inherent in all of creation. It would reveal the ghoulish scene taking place under our noses. It would expose the inherent *evil of nature*. Again, only Becker could deliver this truth with the *real* force it warrants:

> What are we to make of a creation in which the routine activity is for organisms to be tearing others apart with teeth of all types – biting, grinding flesh, plant stalks, bones between molars, pushing the pulp greedily down the gullet with delight . . . and then excreting with foul stench and gases the residue. Everyone reaching out to incorporate others who are edible to him . . . not to mention the daily dismemberment and slaughter in 'natural' disasters . . . The soberest conclusion . . . is that the planet is being turned into a vast pit of fertilizer.[18]

Our fellow creatures may come to us plastic-wrapped, and we may use fancy cutlery and fancy manners in the process, but we too are biting and grinding and pressing dead flesh down our gullets. Becker is right in saying that we cannot afford to get boxed into a corner with the full truth about reality. Bellow's Mr Sammler was stunned one day when he finally saw that "reality was a terrible thing, and that the final truth about mankind was overwhelming and crushing . . . that life was really a singular state of misery . . . that the answers were horrible." We would become psychologically and emotionally assaulted by too large a dose of truth. That would have doomed us to extinction long ago. Through the character of Maria Icaza, in *The Eighth Day*, Thornton Wilder gives a chilling description of the terrifying nothingness of life. In that book, the character John Ashby has trouble defending himself from too much reality: it has crept into his dreams:

> You are having the dream of universal nothingness. You walk down, down, into valleys of nothing, of chalk. You stare into

pits where all is cold. You wake up cold. You think you will never be warm again. And there is *nothing* – and this nothing laughs, like teeth striking together. You open the door of a cupboard, of a room, and there is nothing there but this laughing. The floor is not a floor. The walls are not walls. You wake up and you cannot stop your trembling. Life has no sense. Life is an idiot laughing. Why did you lie to me?[19]

The idiot laughing! How could one ever want a more perfect description of creation? To wake up from our dream and from our lies would be to see the idiot, the nothing, the teeth striking viciously and mindlessly together. In waking up, we would see chaos. Any laughter would be the hopeless sound that one hears from those sentenced to the gallows. We must deny the truth.

Modern physicists are adding credence to this unromantic portrait of life by offering impressive evidence that the natural world is perfectly and absolutely chaotic. In fact, a new school of quantum physics is building on the premise that chaos and pure chance underlie the workings of the universe itself. Some are challenging Einstein's previously accepted dictum that order exists in the universe.[20] There now seems good reason to suspect that all matter, at all levels, is fundamentally unpredictable and chaotic. All we seem to manage is the *illusion* of order. Without artificial methods for translating chaos into the semblance of order, we would soon encounter a cosmic bedlam where no reasons could be found for anything.

An intelligent and highly conscious animal would be relegated to lunacy if surrounded by the *reality* of chaos. Successful coping and survival became dependent upon our being able to convert chaos into imagined order. That kept us from this ultimate madhouse and allowed us to use our magnified brain capacity to our advantage. Additional support for this idea comes from researchers who are finding that the human being does, in fact, have extreme problems with randomness. Lee Ross, a psychologist at Stanford University, believes that certain types of paranormal belief can be traced to the human brain's difficulty in coping with the perception of random events.[21]

Therefore, the problem with evolution's first design of the big brain went beyond the serious emotional consequences associated with death awareness and the perception of other stress-generating realities. Without at least the illusion of order, nothing else makes sense. The world would have been mental pandemonium. Surrounded by randomness and tumultuous chaos, our early ancestors would have been, as Ortega y Gasset phrased it, "shipwrecked by reality." It is unlikely that they could have coped with the anxiety and confusion engendered by so many events and happenings for which there was no explanation. Their natural inclination would have been to focus on their immediate problem which was their ignorance of the world in which they found themselves. We know ourselves how difficult it is to concentrate our energies when even relatively minor problems are unresolved. One can only try to imagine how impossible it would have been for these creatures to tackle each apparently illogical day with logic and pure intelligence. Their brains would have shut themselves down like an overloaded computer. They would have been rendered unproductive to the extent that their very survival would have been unlikely. In *The Ghost Dance*, Weston La Barre writes that "religion is what man does with his ignorance."[22] In fact, all paranormal self-transcendence is what we do with our ignorance. Ironically, this "ignorance" is the result of an intelligent creature being able to ask questions for which there is only an unwanted answer – life is meaningless in its fundamental chaos. So, we do our best to parry the dangerous and unnerving knowledge that derives from the unblinded eye.

Magic, religion, and all forms of reality distortion are simply species-specific responses unique to the human animal. These act in our service. Paranormal belief did a great deal for us: it did nothing less than save us from extinction. In his book *Mankind Behaving*, J. R. Feibleman speaks vividly about the *adaptive* value of religious paranormal beliefs:

> Theologies are qualitative response systems which promise survival. Irrespective of their truth or falsity (and since they conflict, no more than one of them can be true), the overwhelming statistics as to their prevalence indicate that they are necessary for some need-reduction in the individual. The need is, of course, the need for survival, for ultimate security . . . Religion is an effort to be included in some domain larger and more permanent than mere existence.[23]

Birth was given to the paranormal believer in a brilliant evolutionary tactic that allowed intelligence to remain the mechanism for our survival. It was to be a maneuver quite unlike the usual adaptations observed in nature. It was necessary for us to use an amplified state of consciousness to function within the realities of our situation. Simultaneously, however, it was also essential that we avoid perceiving reality for what it was – chaos followed by oblivion. That is as difficult as asking someone to see and be blind at the same time. We had to retain all the advantages of our new intelligence while being usefully "ignorant" enough of the same reality of which we needed to be aware. That sounds, and is, contradictory. But that is exactly what was required – namely, a creature of contradictions, of opposites. We became the genius ignoramus, the wise fool, the truth-hating seeker of truth, the chimera as we now exist. We became what Bellow (Mr Sammler) refers to as the "wretched, itching, bleeding, needing, idiot genius of a creature."

Paranormal belief was the solution to the problems that plagued evolution's initial attempt to use intelligence as the primary source of survival. The *perception* of reality had to be radically altered. This is where Bergson does so fine a job in *Two Sources of Morality and Religion* of describing the specific means by which intelligence was modified by evolution to include a tandem brain function. He labeled this regulatory ability "counter-intelligence" and described it as "a defensive reaction against what might be depressing for the individual, and dissolvent for society in the exercise of intelligence."[24] In those brilliant words, we have the key to unlock the greatest mystery of our species. Quite simply, counter-intelligence rescued us from the psychologically enfeebling quality of pure intelligence. This additional capacity gave us the means to believe what otherwise would have been impossible to believe with pure intelligence alone. We could override reason and logic and thereby bias our perceptions of reality. It enabled us to live and operate in the clutches of our real condition while also believing our condition to be something different from what it actually was.

When unfettered intelligence reached that developmental stage where it threatened to wreak emotional havoc on us, a need became established for myth-making. These myths had to be paranormal ones that could, as Ortega y Gasset stated in *Revolt of the Masses*, serve as "scarecrows to frighten reality away." We would be able to utilize our wonderful mental machinery while staying secure in what Rilke described as our redefined world. Bergson writes that our counter-intelligent paranormal fictions would "guard against certain dangers of intellectual activity without compromising the future of intelligence."[25] He also uses the term "counterfeit experience" in describing the new innate cognitive process that "confronts intelligence and stops it from pushing too far the conclusions it deduces from a true experience."[26] So, evolution even armed us with the brain-level weapons to override, discount, or reshape the *experiences* that would have derived from pure intelligence alone. We became, for Bergson, "the only creature endowed with reason, and the only creature to pin its existence to things unreasonable."[27] The chimera was born!

Religion emerged, giving us a blanket of "divine" insulation. Also appearing was the menagerie of other "voluntary hallucinations," as Bergson called them. We had shelter and, from then on, our lives became an exercise in "theodicy." This, according to Peter Berger in *The Sacred Canopy*, meant that we could rationalize and ritualize our ways into a safe interpretation of the cosmos. And we were now able to do this despite the facts, despite the reality that had earlier monopolized pure intelligence. We had now boarded the wobbly wings of illusion with our big brains and our necessary self-deceptions to fly toward a splendored but uncertain future. Our lies about reality would become the welcomed beacon to guide us through the same psychologically treacherous reality. Whether it was all worth the evolutionary effort is a question we shall raise later. Passingham concluded his discussion in *The Human Primate* by predicting that, if offered the option to become a human, a "rational chimpanzee would take one look at human society and turn down the offer." Amplified intelligence certainly had, and has, its problems.

## The path of normal insanity

Possibly without knowing it, the singer-songwriter Jimmy Buffet describes exactly our paramount requisite. In his 1977 *Changes in Latitude, Changes in Attitude* album, he sings: "If we weren't all crazy, we would all be insane." The contradiction here is again apparent, but that seems to be how our brains work (and do not work). Without "crazy" belief systems we would have become insane and, in all probability, extinct. In *Orthodoxy*, G. K. Chesterton emphasizes what an exception we are to the rest of the animal kingdom. He writes that if it is not true that we are a divine being that fell, then we can be certain that we are an animal that went entirely off its head at one point. I harbor serious doubts that we are the way we are by falling from a divinity. Our species was destined to lose its head when it abandoned the original evolutionary prototype of the human brain. We had to become able to twist and distort reality in order to shield ourselves from our own intelligence. Somehow, we had to find a way of becoming crazy so that we would not go insane.

Before we unravel all the terms that can describe abnormal behavior, let us ask if it is possible that the paranormal belief adaptation forced us to become a genuinely insane species. The answer is an important one and it has critical implications for the reformulation of an entire class of mental disorders which will be discussed later. At first glance, it sounds like a preposterous question, since we think we know what we mean by insanity. And, we know that insane beings are defined as such because they are acting, thinking, or feeling distinctly differently from the majority of us. So, let us ask a double question. Is it possible that our paranormal belief behavior is sufficient to warrant that we be labeled insane, and can it also be that the majority of a species can be insane?

No one argues more effectively that the human animal is *absolutely* insane than the eminent anthropologist, Melford Spiro.[28] He went so far as to rename our species *homo religiosus* because of the paranormal beliefs – usually "religious" – that are omnipresent in our species. Spiro states that paranormal belief meets all the necessary conditions that permit us to diagnose the paranormal believer as insane. This provocative view is based on the fact that various types of distortion are involved in the adoption and maintenance of paranormal belief systems. He says that "distortion implies the existence of some reality relative to which a cognition is false, a perception that is skewed, an affect that is misplaced." Even though we have come to accept paranormal distortions as generally "normal," he contends that there is good reason to question the sanity of people who harbor such distortions of reality.

In similar fashion to that described earlier, Spiro concedes that these paranormal belief systems are useful defense mechanisms. Since the religious paranormal beliefs to which he refers are typically woven into the fabric of a culture, he labels these belief systems "culturally constituted defense mechanisms." But, even though they may be of some adaptive value, Spiro insists, that does not automatically permit us to call religious and other paranormal belief systems "normal." This can be seen when he asks, "how can we be sure that religious behavior is not abnormal behavior, requiring psychiatric, rather than sociocultural analysis?"[29] Specifically, Spiro details three areas of reality distortion that suggest paranormal beliefs are an "impairment of psychological functioning." These include (a) cognitive distortion in which logically unfounded beliefs are held to be true; (b) perceptual distortion in which stimuli are perceived as something other than what they are; and (c) affective distortion and the hyper-affectivity (or hypo-affectivity) that is often associated with paranormal belief and experience.

Other thinkers have had the vision to recognize the insanity at the root of the human quest for paranormal self deception and reality distortion. Some have highlighted the *necessary* nature of this insanity. Pascal, for example, observes in *Pensées* that we are so *necessarily* insane that not to be afflicted in this way would be simply another version of insanity.[30] If we understand and accept this, we see that our thinking has been back-to-front in psychology. It becomes evident that we should not be talking about normality and mental health as if these implied contact with the *real* reality of the world around us. Rather, we should be asking at what level of illusion we function best. That is, what degree of insanity and reality distortion makes us most "normal." One might ask about any possible joy or comfort that could come to the fully aware person, the one who was not *madly* removed from reality. The answer is that there is none at all to be had. Insanity, as measured by the psychological distance we create between ourselves and chaotic reality, is to be considered "normal" and necessary.

The idea that the human being is dependent on a certain degree of mental disturbance in order to be "healthy" and functional can be traced to the writings of Kierkegaard and Nietzsche. In order to be "normal," Kierkegaard writes, one has to be mentally sick.[31] At best, we can hope for "fictitious health" that allows the human being to "tranquilize itself with the trivial" and thereby escape the reality of our condition. Kierkegaard developed the argument that reality, in all its chaos and incomprehensible happenings, presents the human brain with an extreme amount of possibility. For Kierkegaard freedom, including the freedom of thought and emotion that would allow us to apprehend reality, threatens to overwhelm us with unhealthy levels of possibility. Mental health is nothing more than normal neurosis. By this definition, the "normal" person is one who can conquer freedom, truth, and possibility. In *Sickness unto Death*, Kierkegaard writes that only the "audacity of despair" awaits the person who sees too much possibility and refuses to become one of the normal "sick" slaves to reality distortion and self-deception. One can see how Kierkegaard helped shape Rank's concept that mental health is reliant on a rejection of reality, and that true normality is a matter of achieving ideal illusion. In other words, sanity depends on achieving and maintaining a workable form of insanity in the form of illusion. Nietzsche, too, made reference to the paradoxical nature of the human mind when he spoke of the "neurosis of health" that characterizes us who are "unfaithful to the earth." In *Thus Spake Zarathustra*, Nietzsche infers that our normal insanity is bought at the price of being "poisoned by belief in the superterrestrial" and in whatever else is preached by peddlers of the paranormal. In *Twilight of the Gods*, he asks whether man is a blunder of God, or whether God is only a blunder of man. Even though Nietzsche was disconcerted by the healthy insanity with which most people settle, he did agree that much of human folly was "falsehood in the face of necessity."

Before we get too carried away with reference to the insanity that allows us to be sane, let us keep in mind the important function of self-transcending belief. As Becker writes, our paranormal self-deceptions are "vital lies" that serve as indispensable defenses against a human condition for which there is no other remedy. Becker defined a vital lie as *"necessary* and basic dishonesty about oneself and one's whole situation." He writes:

> these defenses allow him to feel a basic sense of self-worth, of meaningfulness, of power. They allow him to feel that he *controls* his life and death, that he really does live and act as a willful and free individual, that he has a unique and self-fashioned identity, that he is *somebody* – not just a trembling accident germinated on a hothouse planet that Carlyle called a hall of doom.[32]

If paranormal "lies" about reality are vital and serve such a useful purpose, it might seem unjustified to describe them as insane. An important point of clarification is necessary before we can speak later about the types of mental illness that arise when our "religious" needs fail to be met in socially acceptable and efficient ways. Attempts to define behavior that should be deemed abnormal can be roughly divided into three categories. The first and least useful is the cultural relativism definition. This approach only allows behavior to be defined as normal or abnormal on the basis of majority behavior *within* a particular culture of people.

Therefore, if it was customary in a society savagely to club each other on the head for sport, that would be "normal" because it was accepted and endorsed by that particular population of people. Such, by the way, is the practice in certain groups of people living along the Amazon near the border of Venezuela and Brazil. To watch the films made by anthropologists of this behavior is enough to bring on gut-wrenching nausea, and only a diehard cultural relativist would want to call that activity normal. Also, the cultural relativism definition does not permit one to make a qualitative or diagnostic assessment of the belief systems that are to be found among people around the world. Among the Yir-Yiront aborigines of Australia, for example, it is believed that tree spirits are responsible for human fertilization. Some of us might be tempted to label those beliefs as erroneous distortions of reality and to think up a good birds-and-the-bees talk for these people. However, by strict cultural relativism definition, those beliefs are "true" because they are true for those people. You can see how a serious study of paranormal belief systems would go nowhere with such a choice of definition. This model does not allow one to use the term reality with any confidence or to say that someone might be removed from a more stable reality.

The second method by which one can try to label behavior as normal or abnormal is the absolute method. You may have surmised that Melford Spiro was employing this definition when he concluded that religious and most other types of paranormal beliefs are insane. This method does allow one to speak of a reality that exists whether one likes it or not. Further, it permits one to speak of certain realities of the human condition that are in place, whether we try to believe our way around them or not. The absolute definition enables us to judge behavior according to absolute criteria. Therefore, it is possible to describe the majority as insane if their behavior and/or beliefs deviate from the realities that would present themselves to the intact and undistorted mind.

The obvious advantage of using the absolute definition of normality and abnormality is that we can go in where angels fear to tread. We can study such things as paranormal belief without having to submit to the "that's just the way things are" motto of the relativists. One can say that death means you die. One can say that a tree is a tree. If we meet someone who claims that his wife has just had twin girls fathered by a large gum tree, we can say that we have a distortion of reality on our hands. If we find an entire culture with children named after their parental trees, we can say that the whole lot of them are out of touch with reality in that respect. It is only then that we can really study a phenomenon like paranormal belief and ask why it is that these people are distorting reality.

Answering the question is one primary purpose of this book. Once we determine the value of what we have finally established as distortions, we can ask even better questions. For example, what is the result of people having too much or too little reality-transcending belief? Also, what cultural conditions best foster the type of paranormal belief that we need most? Can we learn anything about the nature of paranormal belief that can help us understand and treat certain types of mental illness? These and other important questions depend on our ability to speak of a reality against which we can gauge the distortions that paranormal beliefs represent.

What disturbs many people about the absolute definition is that they think their beliefs are automatically deemed to be false since the beliefs defy logic and reason. I do not believe anyone was ever made pregnant by a tree. But how can I know that? As a Roman Catholic I used to believe that I would burn for an eternity upon my death if I deliberately prevented my wife from getting fertilized by me. That did not sound at all pleasant, but my paranormal sponge soaked it up. Not surprisingly, I also believed I could avoid such a harrowing eventuality if I admitted my action to a specified person (the priest) prior to my death. I also believed wholeheartedly that I would burn in eternal fire if I ate meat on a Friday. I now hear that people no longer spend an eternity in fire for eating meat on Fridays. Yet, I cannot help thinking back on the many Saturdays when I rushed to confess about the bologna and ketchup sandwich I could not resist the day before. I usually hoped I would not die before getting to the 3 p.m. confession. Is that absolutely insane or absolutely insane? The problem is that we are not *entirely* sure.

When one adopts absolute criteria for analyzing paranormal belief, one puts oneself in the awkward position of making judgments about the veracity of those beliefs. Since paranormal beliefs, by their very nature, are in defiance of observable and verifiable evidence, we often end up treating all paranormal beliefs as equal. The gods are tossed into the same basket with astrology, the channeled spirits, UFOs, Bigfoots, black cats, premonitions, bent spoons, and purple people-eaters. Most people resort to the built-in safeguards that all paranormal beliefs have, namely that one cannot *disprove* them. In a sense, absolutists who study paranormal belief systems from a scientific perspective are taking a "leap of non-faith" (as opposed to Kierkegaard's "leap of faith" when he eventually found religion). Again, we know that the 2,000 or so "gods" contradict each other in how they supposedly created and govern the world. Anyone with any mathematical background can quickly decipher that they cannot all be "true." That is, if they all contradict each other, you know that no more than one of those could be the one *true* story.

The absolutist might look at the clashing and contradictory nature of the 1,999 "false" belief systems and ask why we should think that there is even one true story in the bunch. Of course, one could look at any particular god and establish the statistical probability that one is the true one. In each case, the probability would be close to zero. Unfortunately, everyone would find out that the chances of any particular belief system being the *true* one was approaching statistical impossibilty. The absolutist paranormal investigator usually refrains from calling these beliefs "false" and forges on in faithlessness to see how far he/she can go in a scientific study of these beliefs. This does not mean that the absolutist is renouncing the possibility that some paranormal claims may eventually be shown to have some validity. That not forthcoming, however, they usually *act* as if they are distortions of their absolute definition of reality. An absolutist like myself, who also happens to be a clinical psychologist, would then take the liberty of making a faithless diagnosis of insanity if someone seems to be laboring under massive distortions of reality. The point here is that such absolutist judgments are, in fact, a liberty. The ghost of my ferocious fifth grade nun may be watching me as I write and I may soon be dancing on the hottest coals of hell fire for the vasectomy I had a while back. All an absolutist psychologist studying paranormal belief can say is that these beliefs are *probably* a form of absolute insanity. He or she moves on with modesty and bated breath, hoping not to be embarrassed by the discovery of human tree births or pits of burning Friday meat-eaters.

To complicate matters more, we must now say that paranormal belief does not usually constitute *real* mental illness. It is only absolute insanity. To understand this paradoxical concept, one needs to look at the third way by which we can define behavior as "abnormal." This final definition is the clinical one, the method by which mental health professionals typically decide that someone is mentally disturbed or not. Clinical insanity, or mental illness, is the unfortunate type that is associated with conscious psychological suffering. Terms such as "neurotic" and "psychotic" find their way into the vocabulary of psychologists attempting to label the myriad of clinical mental disorders. Clinical mental disturbance can include any one of a wide range of disturbances, including depression, anxiety states, obsessive-compulsive disorders, paranoia, dissociative and somatoform disorders, the schizophrenias, and so forth. The list of clinical problems that beset our species is regrettably long and contains a sad number of disorders for which we have no effective therapeutic interventions. Some of these will be discussed later in light of new understandings and treatments that emerge from an analysis of the paranormal belief imperative.

With the above terminological distinctions in mind, it is now possible to reapproach the concept of normal insanity and see how it is not only feasible but essential for the human being to be simultaneously normal and insane. The need to be absolutely insane believers was part of the fallout of the collision between reality and a high degree of self-aware intelligence. Again, this need is "insane" because belief in the impossible and unbelievable requires a distortion of the world as it would otherwise appear to our rational selves. When we threw reality out of the window in an effort to eliminate chaos, we had to rely on both sense and nonsense in comprehending the world. Once that transpired over evolutionary time, we became "necessarily mad" in the *absolute* meaning of the word. However, the counter-intelligent faculties that meshed with and regulated pure intelligence were protecting our species from clinical madness. Therefore, what Pascal is really saying is that we are all so necessarily *absolutely* mad, that not to be *absolutely* mad would be another form of madness – clinical madness. Buffett's marvelous lyrics should then read "if we weren't all *absolutely* crazy, we would all be *clinically* insane." "Normal neurosis" and "normal insanity" as the terms are used here should actually read "normal absolute neurosis" and "normal absolute insanity."

As Spiro has shown, paranormal belief must be described as a form of insanity by strict *absolute* definition since serious reality distortion is involved. The behaviors and rituals associated with these beliefs would, in kind, also carry the label of absolute insanity. When Kierkegaard speaks of "normal cultural pathology" he means pathology in the absolute sense. Similarly, when Freud describes the "pathology of whole cultural communities,"[33] he is also describing absolute pathology. Absolute insanity was the ideal and intended compromise that evolution devised when pure intelligence threatened to bring reality into terrifying focus. We became unleashed from the confines of rationality, an event that ushered in the irrational. It became ever easier to prefer the supernatural to the excessively real Normal.

Eric Hoffer spoke of the human capacity to escape the rational and the obvious. Our refusal to see reality has created what he called our "distaste for facts and cold logic." Further, he cleverly observed how "it is startling to realize how much unbelief is necessary to make belief possible."[34] That is, not only have we become creatures that can believe in what is not real, but we are creatures that are very skilled at *unbelieving* what is real. Through that evolutionary adaptation, our species became capable of healthy or "normal insanity," which guarded us against cognitive overload and eventual real (clinical) mental disturbance.

Freud took a cynical view of the "schizophysiology" (Bergson's term) that is built into our species and expressed as paranormal belief. Psychological historians consistently comment on Freud's personal vendetta against religion. This led him to turn his otherwise potent insights about our appetite for illusion into vengeful denunciations of religion. However, by equating religion and other self-deception with childhood neurosis, he let his emotions destroy his perspective. In fact, he lost an appreciation for the inherent value of self-deceptive cognitive strategies. He wrongly proclaimed them remnants of "the ignorant childhood days of the human race . . . which the civilized individual must pass through on his way from childhood to maturity."[35] Freud and his followers were also misguided in trying to tie the roots of the religious motive to the family and the even more errant notion of Oedipal relationships. Furthermore, the Freudian position views paranormal believing as a *maladaptive* escape from reality. This line of thinking becomes translated into therapeutic strategies that attempt to strip away these and other defenses against reality. Psychoanalysis truly does become what one critic called a confession without absolution. That is why psychoanalysis is typically found to be the least effective means by which to treat most clinical disorders. In chapter 6, we shall examine those clinical neuroses that represent failed efforts to order reality and satisfy the paranormal belief imperative. My intention will also be to show how the therapist must use, rather than expose and inhibit, our natural inclination to prevent cognitive confrontation with the realities we need to escape.

The extent to which beliefs are *useful* to us is determined by the mechanism for transmitting these beliefs. In the case of the human being, that mechanism is culture. A chapter is devoted to the manner in which culture helps us to defeat reality with normal insanity. Before we do that, however, we need to analyze the amazing ability upon which culture and its belief systems are founded. For culture to propagate belief systems effectively, it must be able to take full advantage of an extraordinary evolutionary adaptation that makes counter-intelligence of all sorts possible. That is the most fascinating of all human characteristics, namely *suggestibility*. Without that special capacity, the unbelievable would never become believable. We would not have survived our collision with reality. It is necessary to understand the role that suggestibility and hypnotizability play in our everyday lives and the cultural dissemination of self-transcending belief. That will enable us to forge a new theoretical model for mental health and mental illness at both the individual and the collective level.

# 3  *Suggestibility and Waking Hypnosis*

It is not sufficient merely to state that counter-intelligent brain processes emerged to combat the intrusion on reality made by pure intelligence. That alone cannot give us a full appreciation of the mechanisms underlying paranormal self-deception. Although evolution did manage to consummate the biological miracle of paranormal belief, we need to gain a deeper understanding of the cognitive invention that reshaped our mental operations so dramatically. After all, it is no small accomplishment to get the most intellectually superior of all beings to believe the impossible, to deny the blatantly obvious, and still to carry on with enough wit and self-conviction to flourish as a species. Some help is needed to internalize and genuinely *believe* what is literally out of this world. My own brain had to be uniquely equipped for me to have been capable of sprinting down the street to confess to eating a bologna sandwich so that I would not burn after death. Also, some special intellectual talent has to be in place for certain tribes of south Central Africa to *believe,* and act in accordance with the belief, that their ancestors live on in the bodies of dead hyenas. And surely, some help is needed to believe, as millions of us do, that we can become reincarnated into a future dog, fish, moose, or whatever. If one stands back far enough and with enough objectivity, one certainly has to scratch one's head regarding the brain-level operations underlying these stupendous feats of illogic. Superficially, it would seem that no self-respecting dogs, moose, or even fish, would let themselves go so awry. And in fact, they would not. They would have no need to.

I had a client some years ago who came to me saying he believed a leopard was following him. The mental health team of which I was a member eventually arranged for him to be institutionalized and placed on psychotropic medication. One might ask, however, if my "burn forever for your bologna sandwich" belief did not warrant that I take a bed on the same ward. The answer is no. Another client of mine sought help because she believed she would die if she did not wash her hands every few minutes. But should I not have been the one on the couch for believing I could avoid everlasting agony by confessing my bologna story to a celibate man in a box? Again, no. I was not *really* mentally disturbed. They were. Fortunately for me, I was *absolutely* insane and therefore as healthy as I could be. I had no need to be clinically insane. They did.

Rank himself expressed the *normal* nature of our drive for cognitive error and misapprehension: "With the truth, one cannot live. To be able to live one needs illusions . . . this constantly effective process of self-deceiving, pretending and blundering is no psychopathological mechanism."[1] In his own stirring fashion, Rank went on to recount the exact moment of illumination that revealed to him the most fundamental of all human motives. He explains that he suddenly woke from a nap, sat up in bed, and knew then what it was that powered human behavior. It was stupidity! And, of course, he was right. The genius "depository of truth" has to become a "stupid earthworm" in order to remain a genius. The most potentially aware creature must become insanely unaware of many boldly conspicuous aspects of its condition. In describing one of his most severely disturbed clients, a fellow psychologist once said, "You need lots of brains to be that crazy." That is true of our species. It is also fair to say in our case that we need lots of brains to be as "stupid" as we are.

A number of prominent thinkers have alluded to our fondness and preference for ignorance (in the sense of *ignoring*). Bertrand Russell wrote that "men fear thought as they fear nothing else on Earth – more than ruin, more even than death," and contended that it is fear that makes most of us abandon free thought and align ourselves with "ignorance." He spoke of the thought-induced disaster that must be averted at all cost. That feared disaster is that our "cherished beliefs should prove to be delusions."[2] Without question, honest thinking is the worst of all possible tortures for most people. In this vein Konner wrote that there is an alternative to the "typical sort of religious denial that most of our species have embraced throughout most of history." That alternative, he says, is not to think about things, including the nature of the human condition.[3] To do otherwise would be to ask for psychological trouble.

The "ignorance is bliss" adage is an old one and no doubt many painfully aware souls would seriously consider exchanging their troublesome knowledge for even a little "grace" or healthy "stupidity." But that was not meant to be for our species. War was declared as soon as the intellectual Rubicon was crossed and we had to cope with our formidable thought capacities. Not to think was *not* the answer. When we are accused of not thinking, what is usually implied is *selective* non-thinking about certain aspects of our worlds. We still think and perceive, and the reason we can do that is because we have aligned ourselves with the irrational.

Paranormal believing became the antidote to pure intelligence. To become paranormal believers, however, our brains had to evolve the ability to be *suggestible*. We had to become a hypnotic animal. Suggestibility is the lifeblood of the paranormal believer. Without it, human beings would have been unable to find illusory refuge in the comforting arms of absolute insanity. In *Escape from Evil*, Becker writes that we human beings are suggestible and consequently submissive because we are naturally in search of the "magic" that will enable us to transcend the cold darkness of the human condition. Only suggestibility would enable us to attain the state of consciousness that would let us keep our feet on the ground while having our heads in the clouds.

Efforts in recent years to sub-classify suggestibility (e.g., primary, secondary, tertiary, challenge, interrogative, etc.) have done little to focus light on the vital role that suggestibility plays in the everyday mental life of all human beings. However, some creative individuals, such as Erlendur Haraldsson of the University of Iceland, are observing the connection between suggestibility and paranormal believing. In one recent study, he found a clear relationship between level of suggestibility and extent of belief in paranormal phenomena.[4] That would be expected if suggestibility is, in fact, the mental faculty that enables us to engage in paranormal beliefs. In that same study, Haraldsson found a positive correlation between level of suggestibility and "perceptual defensiveness." This latter term refers to "strength of defense mechanisms when faced with threat." Again, one would expect to find such a relationship if I am correct in the view that suggestibility fosters the belief systems that serve to *defend* us from too much reality.

One must try to dispel some of the unwarranted mystery attached to human suggestibility and hypnosis. For example, there is nothing new about these phenomena. It is true that Western psychologists only "discovered" suggestibility-based behaviors in the latter part of the nineteenth century. None the less, suggestibility has been a central feature of the human mind since the dawn of the paranormal belief imperative. Non-Western healers have been making therapeutic use of our innate suggestibility for thousands of years. Western psychologists have largely ignored or underestimated the importance of this fascinating dimension of our cognitive processes. Only now are a few of us trying to catch up with the natives in understanding ourselves as creatures of hypnosis.

Another misconception is that suggestibility and hypnosis are different from one another. You can see that I have been using the terms suggestibility and hypnosis interchangeably. I do that deliberately. It is incorrect to view the hypnotic trance as anything but a dramatic expression of the same suggestibility that influences our thoughts and actions in the so-called waking state. The spectacular nature of the deep hypnotic trance tends to color over the more subtle ways that suggestibility works to alter our perceptual worlds on a permanent and continual basis.

This leads to another misconception that we might discuss, namely that suggestibility is somehow strange or unusual. On the contrary, it is always with us. It represents an indispensable ingredient in what we recognize as consciousness. The same is true of highly elevated suggestibility states. Even though someone in a deep hypnotic trance may appear to be functioning in a manner totally different from a waking person, that is not the case. Stage hypnotists have no problem planting suggestions in their unwary volunteers that have them clucking like chickens and shooting at imaginary pink elephants. That is you and me and the rest of humanity. While we might not act out those ludicrous antics, we are none the less constantly incorporating pre-packaged suggestions that warp our realities in the required manner. We do not see ourselves in the same way we do the people on stage as they act out their silly suggestions. Yet, if the truth be known, the suggestions we act out on our cultural stages are, in most cases, no less a distortion of reality.

Leon Chertok has written about the history of our understanding of what we have come to call hypnosis.[5] He states that we have not come far since the late eighteenth century when claims about hypnosis were regarded with suspicion and even disdain. Even though a considerable amount has been written on the subject of hypnosis, few writers have opened up any new perspectives. As a result, hypnosis is surrounded today by as much confusion and misunderstanding as ever. Chertok even refers to a "taboo on hypnosis" that persists to this day. It is again the result of fear, ignorance, and wild misconceptions about this very human and normal characteristic. This is very unfortunate, as suggestibility and hypnosis hold the key to a new understanding about the workings of the human mind. They contradict the theoretical formulations that now exist concerning the basis for much of human behavior. However, once properly understood, they enable us to rethink the nature of the motives that energize and give direction to human action.

Hypnosis, as an expression of suggestibility, is totally ordinary and explainable in very normal terms. There is nothing magical about it, as many believe. In fact, the more understanding and objectivity one achieves about human belief and behavior, the more one realizes that all of us live under the spell of hypnosis. The suggestions we receive and act out are just as absurd and beyond our control as clucking like chickens and shooting at pink elephants. The only reason we do not see ourselves like those up on the stage is that we are all doing the *same* foolish things, and thus have no means of *absolute* comparison. Sometimes we look at other societies and snicker at their absurd beliefs and behaviors. But every group manages to convince itself that it is not in a similar mental fog and that its beliefs and actions are not equally mindless and ridiculous. It seems to be the very nature of human groups to validate their own belief systems, no matter how fantastic they might be. Simultaneously, we reject those of other groups. The very act of denouncing other systems of belief and related behavior is part of the self-validation process. In that sense, the renunciation of different belief systems serves to fuel and perpetuate the beliefs of one's own group. However, all this is dependent on group members being in a *constant* state of hypnosis.

John Kihlstrom defines hypnosis in his comprehensive review of this subject:

> Hypnosis is a social interaction in which one person responds to suggestions offered by another for experiences involving alterations in perception, memory, and voluntary action . . . these experiences and their accompanying behaviors are associated with subjective conviction bordering on delusion, and involuntariness bordering on compulsion.[6]

Martin Orne, one of the foremost thinkers on the subject of hypnosis, adds to this definition by outlining the primary features of this human ability.[7] These include (a) an altered state of consciousness; (b) a compulsion to follow cues from external sources; (c) the potential to experience as real what are in fact perceptual distortions; (d) by-passing of objective reality; and (e) the capacity to tolerate inconsistencies in logic.

In these definitions, we can see the important part that hypnosis plays in structuring our interpretations of reality. Hypnosis is a state of elevated suggestibility that allows us to achieve and maintain altered perceptions (and even recollections) of reality. As Kihlstrom notes, hypnosis creates in people convictions that resemble delusions and actions that are as automatic and unreasoned as compulsions. We saw in chapter 2 that delusions and misperceptions of reality are essential to our psychological well-being. They represent the "counter-intelligence" that filters the truth out of the perspectives we have of the world around us. Hypnosis is simply the cognitive process that affords us the capacity to translate and re-shape our worst enemy. Again, that enemy is reality, the brute that waits to pounce on the undeluded mind. As such, the healthy person is one who can achieve a satisfactory level of ongoing receptivity to the suggestions that will restructure his or her perceptions. That is another way of saying that optimal mental functioning depends on our ability to *remain* in a state of hypnosis. Only then can we achieve the selective "blindness" upon which we thrive. Only then do we achieve sufficient "ignorance" to ignore what needs to be ignored.

To understand this, we must recognize that consciousness, as we know it, is already an *altered* state. That is, "normal" consciousness is characterized by a built-in reduction in level of consciousness. In our normal waking state, we are not fully awake. Rather, we are in a mild hypnotic trance most of the time.

The recent innovative ideas of Ernest Rossi help to illuminate this seemingly implausible prospect. In writing about the "common everyday trance," he remarks that the human being's "most peculiar blind spot of consciousness is its inability to recognize its own . . . altered states when it is experiencing them."[8] Rossi draws attention to how ordinary human consciousness, in the course of everyday events, is unaware that it is "dreaming" rather than awake. By this he means that it is very difficult to ascertain whether our regular states of consciousness are themselves altered in subtle but significant ways. The everyday trance is a mild hypnotic or autosuggestive state which is the end-result of life-events being filtered through the complex set of ever-present suggestions. We shall see that, although the specific suggestions are group-derived, this trance is actually a form of self-hypnosis. According to Rossi, the common everyday trance should be viewed as a totally natural method of achieving "non-demanding relatedness." In my view we need a relationship to the world that is less "demanding" than one that would result in a trance-free state.

Rossi comments on the failure of mainstream psychologists to study the behavioral manifestations of the waking trance. He none the less cites several philosophers and metaphysical thinkers who have recognized the human being as either semi-conscious, unawakened, sleepwalking, or otherwise only partially in contact with the surrounding world. This same conception of human cognition is echoed by Eric Fromm, who remarks on how loudly one (the "prophet") must call to "awaken man from his customary half-slumber."[9] We became this somnambulistic creature when we crossed the intellectual threshold that forced us to ally ourselves with the irrational.

One of the earliest Western psychologists to express the concept of a "waking hypnosis" was Sando Ferenczi. In 1916, he wrote that "there is no such thing as 'hypnotizing' in the sense of psychical incorporating of something quite foreign from without."[10] He stated that procedures for hypnotic induction did not actually *do* anything to the individual. Instead, Ferenczi destroyed the myth of hypnosis when he spoke of "pre-existing autosuggestive mechanisms" that are universal and ever-present in the human being. That is, we are *normally* predisposed to autosuggestive states, and it is *normal* for us to be and remain in such a state. To Ferenczi, the purpose of this autosuggestive predisposition is to achieve "blind belief and uncritical obedience." That sounds very much like W. McDougall's definition of hypnosis as "acceptance of an idea without logical regard."[11]

In *Group Psychology and the Analysis of Ego*, Freud wrote that the human being inherits a powerful "wish to be governed by unrestricted force."[12] This force is not experienced automatically by us and must, therefore, be cognitively manufactured. Illusion works best in the form of *paranormal* self-transcendence. It provides high-quality untruth which gives us a reassuring sense that we are part of something other than chaotic nonsense and meaninglessness. But neither the earthly nor the unearthly myths and illusions that permeate our lives would be possible if we could not function in an autohypnotic state. We keep coming back to human suggestibility when we attempt to understand the strange blend of sense and nonsense that characterizes human behavior.

Otto Fenichel also saw the importance of suggestion in the everyday lives of people. In an analysis of Eric Fromm's outstanding book *Escape from Freedom*, Fenichel spoke of human beings as "*longing* to be hypnotized" in order to achieve the sort of "magical protection" experienced by children convinced of parental omnipotence.[13] In fact, it makes perfect sense that we need to be in a state of "waking hypnosis" to achieve the magnitude of self-deception and illusion that we see in the average member of our species. A purely rational and critical mind that is solely reliant on empirical verification for its conclusions about the world would be unable to construct *para*normal perceptions. Fromm himself perceived our penchant to escape from the frightening degree of freedom and truth to which unbridled reality exposes us. He saw it as one of our most basic and uniquely human needs to transcend ourselves and reality. We, in a manner of speaking, escape from freedom and reality in order to arrive at a set of beliefs that will enable us to perceive the world as having order, purpose, and meaning.

Fromm, like the psychoanalytic theorists Ferenczi and Fenichel, understood our need to weave an *acceptable* version of the truth about our condition. However, unlike his strictly psychoanalytic counterparts, Fromm viewed myth-making and magical thinking as essential to our general psychological well-being. This is in complete contrast to those schooled in Freudian psychology. For them, paranormal belief, as well as the urge to transfer themselves to the illusion of a safer world, is pathological in nature. The Freudians' cynical view about our escape from reality into paranormal belief and earthly transferences is an extension of their basic "man is evil" assumption. Fromm realized that myth-making and self-transcendence were prerequisites to mental health. In actuality, we are not so much evil as we are afraid. We are more driven to good hiding places than we are to truth or self-awareness.

## Suggestibility and endorphin addiction

The principle of operant conditioning has been used to explain how we come to adopt paranormal beliefs and related rituals. I shall describe this briefly, as it explains *part* of the manner in which paranormal beliefs are acquired. For the uninitiated, operant conditioning is a type of learning that involves reinforce-ment (reward) *after* a behavior has been performed. Reinforce-ment can be anything that the animal finds satisfying or that results in "need reduction."

Imagine a hungry pigeon (with a food need) foraging along a city street. It spots and makes a *random* peck at a bottle cap. Let us say that under that bottle cap we had placed a food pellet. Therefore, the random peck would have been *followed* by reinforcement. Now, the likelihood that the pigeon will peck at the next bottle cap it encounters is increased. If we had taken the time and energy to place pellets under lots of bottle caps, we would soon have a pigeon doing almost nothing but pecking at bottle caps. That is a very simple example of how operant conditioning works. It is the same procedure that is used to teach porpoises to jump through hoops, brown bears to ride a bicycle, and chickens to play tic-tac-toe at carnivals. While, naturally, one could go into much greater depth on the subject, operant conditioning is basically the *shaping* and strengthening of random behaviors as a result of reward that follows those behaviors. The only problem people have in understanding this type of learning comes from the fact that the behavior comes first and is *followed* by reward.

Operant conditioning works with humans, too, and undoubtedly serves to shape much of our behavior. To illustrate this, let me briefly describe how some students once used me as a guinea pig for an operant conditioning experiment. Early in the semester, they conspired to *shape* me so that I would wear blue shirts more often. I did, in fact, have a couple of baby blue shirts in my wardrobe, but blue shirts did not outnumber the shirts of other colors. Furthermore, blue was by no means my favorite color. They agreed that, on days when I wore a blue shirt, they would smile at me more often, ask intelligent questions (as painful as that must have been), and do lots of affirmative nodding when I lectured and answered their questions. On blue shirt days, they even had one or two students come up and compliment me on that day's class. They kept an impressive record of my shirt wearing and did a commendable job of keeping straight faces throughout the semester. I had no conscious knowledge of their scheme. None the less, as they predicted, I came to wear blue shirts more and more frequently as the semester progressed. Blue shirts and I became a standing joke and, to this day, I make a *conscious* effort to wear a variety of colors.

A number of theories about the origin of all types of paranormal belief and ritual revolve around this principle of operant learning. James Alcock is one such person who explains "magico-religious" belief in such a way.[14] If, for example, we human beings have a need to escape from the fear and anxiety associated with death awareness, entertaining the belief that the soul survives physical death would produce reinforcement. Our need reduction would be experienced as rewarding and that same belief would be more likely to be repeated. Alcock notes that reinforcement does not have to follow every response for a behavior to become established. In the above example, that would mean that not every act of belief (if one can call belief an "act") would need to be rewarded with anxiety reduction. In fact, learning theorists have long known that learning can better resist extinction if reinforcement does *not* follow every response. There are a number of "schedules" of reinforcement with which any behavior, including beliefs, can be reinforced. It has been well documented that the "variable ratio" schedule results in the fastest learning, as well as the type of learning that is least likely to die out. On this schedule, the subject does not have any idea of how many responses will be required before reward will be forthcoming. Slot machines are so addictive because they operate on the variable ratio of reinforcement. Alcock makes the case that the appearance of magico-religious beliefs may come about and be maintained by that particular reinforcement schedule.

Other proponents of this learning model explain a variety of specific paranormal beliefs and activities as the consequence of operant reinforcement. In *Magic and Religion*, G. B. Vetter shows that belief in superstition can be understood by operant conditioning. He writes about some of the superstitious beliefs whereby certain ritualistic activities are thought to exert control over nature. These could include anything from rain dances and the planting of women's menstrual blood in efforts to enhance agriculture, to the baseball pitcher's dogged insistence that victory is more possible if he drives one particular route to the ball park. Vetter states:

> In the normal course of events rains usually do fall, plagues run their course, and . . . *in the end*, either the crises are resolved in the material world or the individual finally adjusts himself to the loss of crops or family. . . . *And whatever activities were concomitants of this adjustment process that finally ended the stresses will again be the habits called out the next time similar crises arise.*[15]

Again, behaviors and beliefs increase in frequency if they are associated with reward or the easing of a need. According to this reasoning, the emergence of a rain dance was probably the result of much needed rain *following* an ordinary dance on one or more occasions. That ritual then became a part of the method by which individuals in that society dealt with drought. If later rain dances were *never* followed by rain, that ritual and belief would probably die out in time. But the chances are that once in a while rain will follow in the next day or so, thus resulting in a variable ratio schedule of reinforcement for that belief and activity. Yet according to the strict laws of operant learning, some direct reinforcement would be necessary in order to avoid the extinction or disappearance of those behaviors.

One could spend a great deal of time discussing many other superstitious behaviors that are beyond the rational and "normal" workings of the everyday world. Vetter described a World War II pilot who would not consider embarking on a combat mission if he were not wearing a particular sweater. Other people carry rabbits' feet or charms of various sorts to ensure an extra share of good luck. The list of non-rational behaviors that are operantly conditioned is a long one. A researcher, James Henslin, was especially fascinated with the irrational behavior of people playing dice.[16] He observed all kinds of seemingly bizarre actions that they had acquired. Some would talk to the dice before tossing them. Others would snap their fingers, blow on the dice, put the dice to their ear, and so forth. This too can be explained according to operant conditioning theory. Any behavior that preceded a win (reinforcement) was likely to be repeated. From that point on, only an occasional reinforcement would suffice to keep that behavior intact.

Alcock maintains that operant conditioning is a very powerful force, capable of explaining the entire range of magico-religious beliefs. Prayer, for instance, would be reinforced if it was followed by "success" in the form of escaping danger or getting what one was praying for. Other theorists have added that prayer may, *in reality*, prove of value to the individual. It is well known that excessively high levels of anxiety will interfere with all types of performance. It is very possible that prayer could become conditioned to feelings of confidence and self-assurance, a factor that could reduce anxiety and make people themselves more capable of coping with their situation.[17] When the gods or spirits do not answer prayers, we know that people do not lose their faith. Some say this can be explained by the fact that most systems of religious paranormal belief have bulit-in rationalizations. I might pray for a deity to save my sick child. If the child dies, that might be interpreted to mean that the god wanted to test my faith, or to make me suffer, or to remove the child from earthly suffering. Every *good* paranormal belief system can rationalize away evidence contrary to that set of beliefs. They are thus protected from extinction or unlearning. However, it could also be that, according to the variable ratio schedule, only an occasional "success" is needed to sustain the belief.

Operant conditioning may go some of the way in explaining paranormal belief and ritual. But one must avoid an oversimplified understanding of the remarkable phenomenon of paranormal belief. We can see, for example, that systems of traditional religious paranormal belief often act as a foundation for normative moral behavior. Such belief systems may even come to play a part in the integration and structuring of societies. None the less, I am of the conviction that the most vital functions of religious and other paranormal systems *precede* and are fundamentally separate from those functions that they serve. One reason I say that is because it seems that paranormal belief/experience is a *chemical* process that is rooted in human biology. In chapter 4, we shall see the crucial part that culture plays in directing and orchestrating our belief imperatives. It should become apparent that belief systems do not have as their *primary* purpose the patterning or integration of society. Instead, the essential role of culture is to standardi: e and coordinate our strong natural propensities for belief. Therefore, the acquisition of unworldly belief goes far beyond the simple laws of learning or the part they might play in structuring society. We are *physiologically* programmed to distance ourselves from reality with paranormal beliefs.

We now enter an exciting new area of study that has the potential to permanently alter the way we understand ourselves. It concerns the recently discovered brain opiates and their relationship to paranormal belief and experience. Collectively, these brain opiates are called endorphins. Investigators are beginning to look at the role these play in certain mental disorders that occur in excessively suggestible individuals. For now, however, we need to limit ourselves to the possible way in which endorphins and suggestibility interact to make religious and all other paranormal belief possible in our species.

Initially, researchers were puzzled by the discovery that each person's brain has the capacity to produce an opiate drug. To complicate matters, it soon became clear that our brains produce several chemical opioids. The next step was to discover *why* our brains had evolved the means to manufacture the sort of drug that, on the streets, is illegal. Of course, the reason this class of chemical substance is illegal is that it not only makes one feel very good, but also that it is addictive. But, since endorphins occur naturally, we can put aside fears of being "busted" and get on with the task of determining the *purpose* of opiate production in the brain.

Our understanding of the different brain endorphins is still in its infancy. Many conflicting theories abound, but the degree of interest in these substances is certain to stimulate continued research and innovative theoretical speculation. What I offer here is the theory that one or more of the various brain opiates is crucial to the *learning* of paranormal beliefs. In addition, I believe the "oceanic" feeling that is often associated with religious experience and other reality-transcending states is, in fact, an endorphin "high." Some clues have emerged to support such an unlikely possibility. Beyond that, we do not simply learn self-transcending beliefs in the operant fashion described earlier. By design, we become addicted to paranormal self-deception and reality distortion.

A few words of preparation would help to establish a foundation for this proposal. First of all, we recall that Bergson theorized that the human species evolved a system of "counter-intelligence" which takes the form of religious and related paranormal beliefs. This serves to defend us from the emotional cataclysm that would have resulted from a situation in which creatures surveyed reality with "pure intelligence." This also implies that we developed a biologically-based mechanism for self-deception, one that would not rely solely on the often slow and frequently unreliable laws of ordinary learning. In essence, Bergson was saying that paranormal belief became an innate motivational system. I believe that is the case.

Reality-transcending paranormal beliefs are of such great survival value that, through evolution, we became biologically *predisposed* to believe the unbelievable. As we shall see, these beliefs become organized and receive protection by various cultural groups. But, most importantly, we evolved into creatures that had brain-level inclinations to develop reality-transcending beliefs. Richard Solomon provides a good description of the distinction between acquired and innate motivation systems.[18] He rightly points out that motivational systems which are *innately* organized are those that are of paramount survival to the organism. That is, they represent capacities that the species cannot afford to do without. Many birds, for example, are born with the ability to make the sounds uniquely characteristic of their particular subspecies. No learning is necessary. Most animals, including the human being, are born with the ability to experience hunger which motivates them to engage in food-seeking activities. We humans also have an innate hunger or motivation for paranormal belief. I previously mentioned that paranormal belief is the only truly universal human characteristic (aside from the "low-level" drives for hunger, water, air, etc.). That is one major clue that paranormal belief has a physiological basis. Additional clues come from the brain-level effects that suggestibility has on members of our species.

Amazingly, our brains seem to have the ability to reward themselves when they "spend" some of their naturally occurring suggestibility. For over 30 years, it has been known that certain regions of the mammalian brain can produce extremely powerful sensations of pleasure and overall well-being. Early research in this area involved the implantation of small electrodes into the hypothalamus of rats. It was found that electrical stimulation of parts of that brain structure were reinforcing for the rat to an extraordinary degree. In a number of studies, rats were rewarded with an electrical impulse to that "pleasure center" whenever they pushed a little metal bar. Researchers were astonished to find that the rats quickly lost interest in doing anything except pushing the bar for their brain stimulation. They occasionally stopped for a quick bite and drink of water. But, aside from that,they pushed the bar over and over again, not slowing down even after many thousands of responses.[19]

These early experiments were significant because they demonstrated that the brain had the potential to reward itself in a potent manner that created very fixed patterns of behavior that were resistant to extinction. Furthermore, it was not long before other research on this subject led to another theoretical breakthrough. Specifically, it became apparent that certain *learning situations* were able to activate those same neural tissues in the same manner accomplished by electrical stimulation. It became clear that the brain can reward itself in a highly potent fashion for *learning* certain behaviors. This led to the study of what is now called Intracranial Self-Stimulation (ICSS), namely, the mechanisms by which the brain neurochemically reinforces or shapes itself. The various theories about the specific physiology of this process is beyond the scope of this book. The specialist wanting an in-depth overview on this subject is referred to the work of Ronnie Halperin and Donald Pfaff.[20] I would like to limit a discussion of ICSS to possible means by which the human brain chemically rewards itself for paranormal believing.

The manner in which suggestibility, self-transcending belief/ practice, and endorphins interrelate appears to be as follows. We are born with the biological tendency to experience suggestibility, in much the same way we are born with the tendency to experience hunger. Human suggestibility manifests itself early in life and normally peaks somewhere between 9 and 12 years of age. From a very young age, we have the potential to override logic, reason, and critical thinking capabilities. Suggestibility, like any other innate motivational system, provides a "tension" which the animal may or may not experience consciously. Unlike hunger or thirst, the experience of suggestibility may not be "conscious" or recognizable to the individual. That would explain why we are not immediately aware of suggestibility, or for that matter, the many types of paranormal self-deception in which we necessarily engage.

Even though we come into the world as suggestible creatures, it is not enough simply to be suggestible. That would be as ridiculous as saying it is sufficient for an animal to be hungry.

Just as hunger must be satisfied, so too must our suggestibility. In a sense, one has to "do something" with one's suggestibility. It has to be satisfied by becoming attached to something. That is, one has to become suggestible *to a target*. More specifically, one's suggestibility needs to be absorbed by a cognitive target. Since suggestibility evolved to enable human beings to believe the unbelievable, it stands to reason that suggestibility is best absorbed by something unbelievable. By "unbelievable" I mean a cognitive set or belief that distances one from the true order and nature of reality.

Evolution had to address the problem that effective reality-transcending beliefs are, by necessity, unbelievable. The rational part of our mental processes stood to detect and "spoil" the necessary nonsensical beliefs deriving from suggestibility. A means was needed by which the brain could receive so lavish a reward that the individual would ignore and override any rational objections to the cognitive nonsense. We became an animal that had to retain rational capacities to enable us to cope with what was real. But, at the same time, we had to be so richly rewarded for hitching our suggestibility to non-rational beliefs that we would actually give preference to them. There was no way that external rewards, offered as operant reinforcers, could convince us to ignore the nonsensical and irrational nature of our beliefs. This is true despite the fact that there are many external social rewards for adopting socially sanctioned paranormal beliefs. The emotional relief one felt by believing in reality-transforming phenomena (e.g., life after death) was also not enough. Apparently, an extremely powerful mechanism of reward was necessary to enable us to ignore and live with the distortions of reality that defied our rational capabilities. An internal system of reward was necessary, one by which the brain could make itself chemically "high." I believe that the function of one or more of the brain endorphins is to reward the brain for behavior that taps the person's level of suggestibility.

Socially sanctioned paranormal beliefs, usually "religious," undoubtedly absorb most of the free suggestibility of which I speak. However, many other human practices lead the brain to reward itself for engaging in behavior that requires one to employ suggestibility. These include faith healing and placebo responses of all types, transcendental meditation, externally-induced hypnotic trance, acupuncture, and so on. Brain endorphin levels appear to increase significantly when people engage in any of these practices.

We know that suggestions, like those implanted during hypnotherapeutic procedures, are able to reduce perceived sensory pain, as well as the "psychological" suffering associated with painful experiences.[21] We also have evidence that highly suggestible people are more able to tolerate physical pain than less suggestible individuals.[22] It has long been known that opiates, such as those in the endorphin group, have substantial analgesic properties. This is true for both physical and emotional forms of pain. In the light of these facts, it is not surprising that brain endorphins should be singled out as a principal mediating factor in the suggestibility process.

Other related research on this topic comes from Howard Fields and his colleagues at the University of California in San Francisco. He concentrated on the well-known "placebo effect" whereby people feel better simply because they *believe* that something is going to make them feel better.[23] Of course, in a placebo situation, the person is not actually receiving any *real* treatment. A classic example would be a medical doctor who gives a non-active sugar pill to a person experiencing imagined pains of some sort. In his experiments, Fields used naloxone, a drug that neutralizes the therapeutic effects of our naturally occurring opiates. Without laboring over the details of his research, he found that naloxone was able to destroy the placebo effect in people who had previously demonstrated that they were "placebo responders." These researchers concluded that the brain releases greatly increased quantities of endorphins when a person reacts to, or *believes* in, a suggestion such as a placebo. However, only about one-third of people are "placebo reactors." To account for this, Fields and his associates suggested that placebo reactors are those people who have become *conditioned* to release endorphins in placebo-like situations. That again lends credence to the possibility that endorphins, as powerful chemical rewards, can establish and sustain patterns of belief.

Although more research in this area is still needed, evidence is mounting that endorphin release and human suggestibility are closely related. Displays of suggestibility, in whatever form, seem to trigger endorphin rewards. And, since suggestibility is at the heart of self-deception, some innovative researchers are now beginning to investigate the actual physiology of self-deception. When we engage in belief that flies in the face of our own reason and rationality, we are employing self-deception. So far, I have been viewing paranormal beliefs as a biologically-based form of self-deception with regard to the world around us. Harold Sackeim and Ruben Gur have spearheaded some of the research into this tantalizing new area. They regard self-deception as "an *active* process as opposed to a passive organization of beliefs on the part of the self-deceived individual."[24] In addition, they state the four criteria that are necessary for behavior to be called self-deception. They are:

1. The individual holds two contradictory beliefs.
2. These two contradictory beliefs are held simultaneously.
3. The individual is not aware of holding one of the beliefs.
4. The act that determines which belief is and which belief is not the subject of awareness is a *motivated* act.[25]

According to their model, it is possible simultaneously to hold two differing beliefs or interpretations of the world. In terms of our discussion of paranormal belief, one might imagine a situation like the one I encountered several years ago in the hills of Luzon in the Philippines, when my wife and I were staying in a remote Igorot village. While there, we had the privilege of being able to speak with these friendly people about their customs and beliefs. The Igorots are known for the very large number of deities in which they believe. In the course of one discussion, I was kindly invited to visit a sacred tree which, for them, was home to certain powerful spirits. Being a hopeless non-believer, I saw a tree. I saw only a tree. Furthermore, I assert now with total confidence that what I saw was, in fact, *just* a tree. One could have made a house or toothpicks from it. I know I could have cursed and ridiculed the tree, or even chopped it down, and those supposed spirits would not have been able to injure a hair on my body. Had my local counterpart done the same, he might have dropped over and died on the spot. Suggestibility (not the spirits and gods) is as powerful as that.

In line with Sackeim and Gur's formulation of self-deception discussed above, I say that my Igorot companion also "knew" that the tree was *just* a tree. After all, I think it is fair to say that trees – be they Filipino, German, or American ones – give us precious little indication that they contain spirits of any sort. For the most part, they stand there and sway in the wind. We have ample evidence of that. My friend's rational thinking abilities were as good as mine. He was just as capable of taking the evidence, or in this case the lack of evidence, and deducing that the tree was simply a tree. So, in a sense, he "knew" and believed that, based on information perceived by his brain. Yet he also held the paranormal belief that the tree was far more than just so many toothpicks or roof supports. So the question then becomes one of how the same brain can entertain beliefs that contradict one another.

I propose that our brains release potent brain endorphins when we channel and *lock up* suggestibility in the form of reality-transcending beliefs. In theorizing that, I am suggesting that the reward is *so* rewarding that we override our critical thinking in favor of the non-rational cognitions that yield the chemical rewards. So, I would agree with Sackeim and Gur that, in a sense, we all know the "truth." That is, on one level, we all weigh up available evidence about the world around us and arrive at accurate conclusions. When the puffy, overweight businessman who masquerades as a religious healer touches and "heals" the sick, the faithful followers "know" that it is a sham. They also believe that a miracle has taken place. Again, the trick is how to know and not know, to see and not see, to believe and not believe at the same time.

A highly peculiar type of mentality results when irrational forces combine with rational ones. Martin Orne calls this "trance logic" and describes the intriguing way it can be seen in people in a deep hypnotic trance.[26] For example, one might give a hypnotized person the suggestion to see a certain friend who is standing in front of him or her. If that individual is highly suggestible, they will be able to hallucinate the presence of their friend. Trance logic can be observed by bringing in the real friend and situating that person next to the unreal friend. Instead of disclaiming the imaginary friend, the hypnotic subject accepts both friends as real. They usually express mild confusion when confronted with the logical contradiction of having two identical but separate friends. Still, they have remarkably little difficulty in maintaining two completely contradictory beliefs.

The common everyday trance affords all of us the ability to employ trance logic. That is how we can simultaneously accommodate the normal with the paranormal. Ours may not be as spectacular as the trance logic seen in deeply hypnotized people. None the less, the same mental processes are at work.

The behavior of hypnotic subjects also tells us that, at one level, they "know" what is real and what is unreal. The prominent psychologist, Ernest Hilgard, illustrated this with a subject he had hypnotized and made "deaf" by use of suggestion.[27] Once the person's hearing had been removed, all auditory tests indicated that the person was not receiving or processing any auditory information. However, Hilgard made the following statement to the "deaf" person: "Although you are hypnotically deaf, perhaps some part of you is hearing and processing the data at some level. If this is the case, lift the index finger of your right hand." In response to those words, the finger rose. The subject could hear and not hear at the same time.

Hilgard also demonstrated this astounding capacity to accommodate opposing information by using hypnotized people who had been subjected to physical pain. In one case, he immersed one of the individual's arms into a tub of circulating ice water. Few of us could tolerate the pain that such extreme cold produces. Yet, through hypnotic suggestion these individuals became immune to pain. Even after sustained exposure to the ice water, they showed and reported no signs of physical discomfort. However, when Hilgard asked them if "at some level" they knew that they were experiencing pain, they responded affirmatively.

Suggestibility enables us to feel pain and not to feel it at the same time. Hilgard proposed that each of us has a cognitive structural system that he labeled a "hidden observer." This, he said, is that "hidden part" of the person that continues to "know" what is happening in reality, even though the person may also believe in something other than objective reality. Hilgard has gone on to develop what is called a "neo-dissociative" theory about the structure of human consciousness. As such, he believes that true and rational perceptions can become "dissociated" from those we accept through the process of suggestion. That is, they are processed in a "parallel" fashion with considerable independence from one another. This implies that we are able to process two separate streams of information despite their complete incompatibility.

Differences between the left and right hemispheres of the brain may further enable us to understand our ability to simultaneously retain contradictory beliefs. Research in this area is adding another dimension to the endorphin reward model that I have just proposed. Specifically, the brain's "asymmetry" (i.e., independent functionings of the two sides) can help to explain the immensely illogical paranormal beliefs that survive all reason and contrary evidence.

It is generally accepted that the two hemispheres of the brain have different, albeit overlapping, functions. As has been found, the left hemisphere is largely involved with logical thought and tends to process incoming information analytically. Verbal comprehension and language ability is thought to be one important left brain function. In contrast, the right hemisphere is the seat of intuition and "synthetic" information processing. Other functions considered to be localized in the right hemisphere include emotion, spatial ability (i.e., the ability to perceive the "whole" of a situation), musical ability and rhythmic sense, imaginative specialization, and what might loosely be called "creativity."

Herbert Fingarette was one of the first researchers to propose that human self-deception is made possible by the differing functions of the left and right hemispheres of the brain. He based his hypothesis on evidence that came from people who had split-brain (cerebral commissurotomy) operations.[28] These are individuals who needed operations that involved the severing of the corpus collasum, the thick bundle of nerve fibers that connects the left and right hemispheres. Such people do, in fact, show a variety of curious behavior, and the interested reader will have no trouble finding a mountain of recent literature on this subject. Of particular relevance here is the finding that one hemisphere seems able to "keep things" from the other. In fact, R. W. Sperry has provided ample data that indicate that split-brain people have two largely independent streams of consciousness.[29] A well-known researcher, Robert Ornstein, also believes that the left and right sides of our brain employ very different cognitive styles. Ornstein specifically theorizes that self-deception in human beings is the result of the right brain *blocking* certain information from entering the left brain.[30] He argues that this forms the physiological basis for all forms of self-deception, including repression and the entire range of cognitive defense mechanisms.

There now seems good reason to suspect that self-deception in the form of paranormal belief may work in a similar manner. As mentioned, the left hemisphere processes information in a logical and analytical fashion. That probably resembles the "pure" intelligence of which Bergson spoke, the type of intelligence that would lead us to become terrorized by "too much reality." Sackheim and Gur report on an innovative line of study which is showing that split-brain patients can hold two contradictory beliefs and be unaware of one of them.[31] That is, one hemisphere can inhibit the other from receiving information about beliefs or conclusions about the nature of the world. In light of what has been said so far about the dangers of seeing things too clearly, there may be good reason why one side of the brain should not share certain beliefs and perceptions with the other. Although far more studies are needed to corroborate these initial findings, the brain-level mechanisms for paranormal self-deception may be coming into focus.

A brief summary of how the hemisphericity model works regarding paranormal belief may be as follows. Self-deception may, as Ornstein postulated, involve the right hemisphere blocking certain information (in the form of beliefs) from reaching the left side of the brain. For example, the logical and reality-based left brain would not be able to believe that a tree contained spirits. It would also not accept that tree spirits make women pregnant. Nor would it accept, as I was once told (and believed) that, by saying the words "Jesus, Mary, Joseph," seven years would be taken off one's post-death sentence in a holding place called purgatory. I once knocked off a full 15,000 years from my purgatory sentence in a single guilty afternoon. However, my left brain was not behind that bout of absolute lunacy. Left brain beliefs about the world are empirically based and derive from direct evidence. It would be quite unlikely that the left brain would ever arrive at beliefs and deductions that are as unfounded in *reality* as those that make up our paranormal beliefs.

Therefore, we have to suspect that the right brain is home to the paranormal believing process. This possibility is strengthened by a sizeable body of research showing that suggestibility and hypnotic susceptibility may be predominantly a right brain function.[32] That is a very exciting discovery, given that suggestibility underlies paranormal types of belief. It also fits Ornstein's theory that self-deception is a consequence of the right brain withholding information from the left. Regarding paranormal beliefs, then, the right brain is probably withholding belief information that (because it is paranormal) is illogical and unfounded empirically. If that information was passed to the left hemisphere, there would be the risk that the left brain would recognize it as literal nonsense. If those belief data spent much time in the left hemisphere, that belief could be effectively diminished or punctured completely. That is not to say that right hemisphere belief information is not shared *at times* with the left brain. In fact, that is almost certainly the case given that we are able to verbalize (a left brain function) our beliefs. I was also able to verbalize "Jesus, Mary, Joseph."

Another of Sackeim and Gur's criteria for self-deception is that *motivation* determines which one of our contradictory beliefs about reality will be in our awareness. There are undoubtedly times when we would experience motivation to have our paranormal beliefs available to the left brain. This would tend to be social motivation when there was a need to mutually reinforce the existing system of paranormal beliefs. When some of us attend church services, for example, the left brain must have a certain amount of access to the irrational right brain belief data that are the product of suggestibility. This must be the case, as church attendance typically involves the verbal communication and comprehension of the paranormal beliefs binding that religious group.

Yet anyone who has ever had an objective look at a church service realizes that "services" are basically group hypnosis sessions. When the right brain passes dangerously inaccurate paranormal belief data to the left hemisphere, for whatever purpose, it seems to exert another important influence. It deepens the "normal" hypnotic trance, thereby reducing the critical thinking capabilities of the left hemisphere. That allows the left hemisphere to utilize language in an attempt to keep most people's beliefs the same, thus avoiding social bedlam. Thank god for hypnosis!

As an additional safeguard for our paranormal beliefs, it is unlikely that the right brain allows much time-sharing of the irrational paranormal methods of construing reality. In that respect, it is probable that even avid paranormal believers are not *aware* of their beliefs most of the time. Too much left brain logic and reason disturbs the harmony between the contradictory beliefs we necessarily hold about the world. We were meant to *feel* beliefs (right brain), not think about and analyze them (left brain).

Much more research is needed to increase our sketchy understanding of suggestibility and its relation to self-deception and self-transcending beliefs. Still, some very exciting theoretical inroads have been made and we stand on the threshold of a new understanding of our chimera-like species. It is becoming evident that suggestibility and trance play a far greater role in our lives than previously thought. We are even gaining some new insights into the brain physiology of this remarkable process that causes us to become "hooked" on suggestibility-based beliefs and practices.

Still, we have only been discussing the nature of suggestibility and *how* it might work in our curiously evolved brains. We have not yet tried to account for the *context* of our beliefs. We are, it seems, hypnotic creatures, who rely on suggestibility for our cognitive flight from reality. But, who or what is it that does the actual suggesting to us? We have the inborn capacity to believe the unbelievable, but from where do our specific beliefs come? What is the actual identity of our hypnotist? What is it that delivers our reality-defying beliefs to us and ensures that these beliefs do not differ so much from one another as to become exposed as nonsense? To answer these questions, we must look at culture and the massive influence it has upon us.

# 4  Culture: The Master Hypnotist

Years ago, I was invited to give a lecture on what I thought human destiny to be. An innovative professor at this particular college was teaching an upper-level course entitled, not surprisingly, *Human Destiny*. His goal was to provide students with various perspectives on this topic from people in a variety of academic disciplines. He specifically asked that I limit my talk to a discussion of human destiny before death, and not to bother giving my opinions about our destiny in a possible afterlife. That suited me, I told him, as I was still trying feverishly to figure out our destiny *in* life. I decided to let the lecture revolve around my special interest in cross-cultural psychology.

I entered a packed classroom of bright and aggressive looking faces. At a glance, I could tell they were loaded with all sorts of theoretical biases about the slippery issue of before-death human destiny. My opening point was that I endorsed the view of the eminent anthropologist, E. T. Hall, who said that our most powerful motive was to *learn our culture*. I rambled on a bit about that idea and then challenged the class to give me a single example of a behavior that was not shaped by culture. They squirmed and squinted as they strained to isolate even one dimension of human behavior that does not carry the distinctive brand of culture. Finally, from the back of the room a couple of meek voices intimated that such behaviors as breathing and the beating of the human heart were free from culture's stamp. I was willing to concede that much, but I knew from their now glassy eyes that I had them. They were mine for the rest of the hour. I went on to accuse them, and myself, of being veritable zombies of culture, robots and puppets of culture, even absolute morons of culture. They did not fight back. They could not. I was right and, in their dazed silence, they begrudgingly agreed. After class, one thoughtful student came up to me and proclaimed that she wanted to be free, and that included freedom from culture. All I could think of replying was, "I'm sorry." I must admit that I too had never before fully envisioned the all-encompassing grip that culture has on every facet of our lives and our mental constructions of reality.

Indeed, we are products of culture far more than we are products of any other single force that shapes our behavior. Specifically, we are products of the cultural suggestions that bombard and mold us. From birth, we are all branded with the beliefs of our culture. These beliefs, which are permanent and indelible, will influence and direct all our actions. And, of all the beliefs that culture must cultivate in its suggestible members, self-transcending paranormal beliefs are by far the most important. To comprehend culture as a figurative hypnotist and the specific manner by which it controls us with suggestion, we must back up momentarily and consider the nature and purpose of culture. But before we proceed with a discussion of the specific functions of culture, we should first try to figure out what it is we are talking about. Finding a suitable definition of culture is no easy task.

Culture has been called everything under the sun. To make matters worse, there is very little agreement between, and even within, the various academic disciplines on this topic. Ronald Rohner recently reviewed the many different definitions of culture that are presently in use today.[1] Despite all the ideological quarreling, he determined that there is unanimity about certain issues concerning culture.

First of all, most agree that culture is a *learned* phenomenon and that what is learned in culture varies greatly from one to another. Rohner's own definition of culture emphasizes the learning component of culture. He describes culture as "the totality of equivalent and complementary *learned meanings* maintained by human population, or by identifiable segments of a population, and transmitted from one generation to the next."[2] Secondly, those who study culture inevitably describe the elements of culture as being *shared*. That is, culture provides its members with certain *common* qualities or characteristics. Therefore, culture automatically refers to something done or endorsed by the majority. In addition, Rohner mentions some general terms that people use to convey the meaning of culture. These include people's "way of life," their "traditions" and what some call the "designs for living." Also, some refer to culture as the unseen provider of the "life scripts" that people act out and mistakenly consider to be the behaviors of their choosing. In actuality, we do not choose those patterns of behavior. Culture does that for us. We follow and obey culture however we may choose to define it.

This latter idea is a difficult one to grasp, for it implies that culture not only *precedes* the individual, but *causes* (or determines) individual behavior as well. The idea that culture precedes the individual is an old one. Aristotle maintained it and also spoke of the power that culture has over the individual. He claimed that only "beasts and gods" could resist becoming enveloped by the imperious dictates of society.

On the issue of causation, I favor a slightly modified version of the "cultural determinism" school of thought concerning the way culture influences us. According to this line of reasoning, culture and the reality of the individual are almost synonymous. The paramount role that culture plays in this respect is captured by Rossides who writes that "culture is not only reality because it *causes* behavior, but it is reality because it *controls* behavior."[3] In this respect, culture has the first and final say in what our thoughts, feelings, and actions will be. Fromm recognized this when he wrote in *Escape from Freedom* that "man's nature, his passions, and anxieties are a cultural product."

Before we look at the actual function or purpose of culture, let us counter the two most common criticisms of cultural determinism. The first maintains that we should not see so many differences between people *within* a particular culture if, in fact, culture was the primary determiner of our behavior. That criticism falls apart when one compares these relatively small differences in behavior to the gigantic differences in behavior that we see *between* cultures. Furthermore, not even the most radical cultural determinist would claim that culture is presented as a single theme that shapes everyone into exact behavioral clones of each other. Culture, as the master hypnotist, offers a variety of suggestions that can be adopted by the subject. To that extent our behavior will vary. All behavior is traceable to this mysterious abstraction we are calling culture. Variation of behavior within a particular culture does not change that fact.

A second criticism of cultural determinism is that it automatically rejects the existence of behaviors that are *universal* in nature. Earlier, I stated that the human being is *almost* totally plastic and malleable. The reason I said "almost" was exactly because there does exist *one* human characteristic that is undeniably universal to all cultures. That, of course, is paranormal belief in its highly diverse forms. Admittedly, many strict cultural determinists would like to sweep that under the carpet and go on believing that it is *only* culture that shapes behavior. My position is somewhat different. Rather than ignore our only universal characteristic, I believe that we should pay especially close attention to paranormal believing. It is, after all, more than coincidence that one particular theme should surface in all cultures of the world. What is more, I believe that this singular universal characteristic holds the key to an understanding of the purpose of culture itself. Individual cultures shape the *form* by which the paranormal belief imperative is expressed. But by no means does the presence of that universal characteristic deflate the argument that culture is what sculptures our realities.

If we continue with this last point, we shall see that the primary function of culture is a response to the human drive for reality transcendence. To do this, one should also view culture as a *cognitive* system. The prospect that culture does, in fact, operate at the cognitive level is being accepted by a growing number of culture theorists.[4] Specifically, culture is a set of *learned* cognitions that are handed down through successive generations. Therefore culture can be seen as a complex set of ideas, beliefs, and meanings that we *must* employ to arrive at some understanding of the world. They represent the suggestions that become accessible to us as we grow into a culture. Such suggestions enable us to create fictitious images of reality.. As such, they are what necessarily stand between us and true reality.

Some people talk about "finding themselves" and being "true to oneself." That talk is so much folly, for all we ever find is culture. Just when we think we have found this self, we open our eyes that little bit more and find that we are still culture in a slightly different wrapping. There is very little freedom to be had from culture. If there is any at all, it is very small and very hard-earned. Each of us becomes culture. Battle as we may, few of us can escape its clutches. We were not intended to escape culture.

Culture, like its primary product, paranormal belief, is good for us. Rather, it *was* good for us.

Culture is the purveyor of normal insanity and counter-intelligence. It is in a manner of speaking the central bank of suggestion that we draw from in order to transform chaos and frightening truths into order and soothing untruths. Culture manufactures the "stupidity" that we need in order to function in this world. Culture is the sacrosanct invention that absorbs the chaos and overwhelming mystery of the universe in which we find ourselves. As such, culture must be understood in the context of our fundamentally theological natures. It is an invention largely in the service of the paranormal belief imperative. Christopher Dawson states:

> While culture is an organized way of life, it is never conceived as a purely man-made order . . . it is founded on a religious law of life, and this law in turn depends on non-human powers towards which man looks with hope and fear, powers which can be known in some fashion but which remain essentially mysterious, since they are superhuman and supernatural.[5]

In their book, *The Biology of Religion*, Vernon Reynolds and Ralph Tanner discuss religious paranormal belief systems and their related behaviors in the context of evolutionary biology.[6] They begin by asking a very important question, namely, how do such beliefs and activities affect the chances of human survival and reproductive success? Reynolds and Tanner go on to argue that many specific religious beliefs and activities represent clear-cut adaptations to certain social and environmental conditions. I agree that the evolution of religion and other paranormal belief systems had very real survival value. My view is different from theirs, however, in that I do not see environmental demands as the *origin* of religious or any other paranormal beliefs. They refer, for example, to the washing rituals that can be found in certain religions, such as Hinduism. Reynolds and Tanner maintain that ritualistic washing, and the beliefs about the religious merits of washing, were a cultural response to poor disease control. Accordingly, the "purpose" of these beliefs and behaviors would be to enhance survival value by reducing the prevalence of disease.

It may be true that, in some cases, religious belief and practices prove to be genetically beneficial to the members of a particular subgroup of our species. But that in no way accounts for the origins of religiosity, nor does it explain why religion should be the necessary means by which such knowledge is disseminated. After all, the great bulk of human information and knowledge about survival methods is passed down through the standard educational channels, usually involving language. If a group comes to understand that washing reduces the risk of disease, there is nothing preventing that learned information from being communicated in *rational* ways. The women of most cultures learn, without religious paranormal beliefs, to put newborn infants to their breasts in order to feed and sustain them. An endless number of other behaviors are passed on without the aid of paranormal beliefs and practices. It is quite unlikely that social or cultural adaptations are the cause of religious or non-religious beliefs and behaviors. It seems more likely that the source of religiosity and paranormal belief is located in the human species itself, and that culture serves a central adjunct function in the employment of these beliefs. This becomes even more obvious when one considers certain human practices that are tied to religious and other paranormal beliefs, but are of very dubious biological advantage.

For example, certain Australian tribes, such as the Walbiri, have a longstanding tradition of splitting their penises. With a sharp stone, the men slice open their penises all the way from the base to the urethra. As a result, the final product, known as a "burra," fans out into a sort of butterfly shape. The semen then leaves the body from near the lower abdomen instead of the penis tip; hardly a prescription for reproductive success. Many young men die as a result of infection brought about by this subincision practice. Now, one would have to think long and hard about any potential genetic advantage that such a culturally-based practice could provide. It would be equally difficult to argue that this development represented any sort of cultural adaptation. The only possibility that presents itself is that there was a need to reduce population size. That does not seem likely, however, given the sparse aboriginal populations and their high infant mortality rate.

The cross-cultural psychiatrist John Cawte has examined possible reasons for this peculiar aspect of this particular aboriginal culture.[7] The explanation that appears to best account for penis splitting is the one that views this practice as an extension of myths surrounding the kangaroo. Debate has taken place about whether or not the kangaroo's penis is, in fact, "split."

Although detailed anatomical inspections reveal that they are not actually split, these aboriginal groups were reportedly of the opinion that they were. In fairness to these people, it should be mentioned that the kangaroo's penis does have a few structural quirks that could lead to the spread of misinformation. None the less, the aboriginal people in mention were thought to assign certain magical or "paranormal" powers to the kangaroo. Such beliefs became imbedded in aboriginal "dreamtime," which is the interesting storytelling procedure they employ for the preserving and passing down of myths. With that in mind, the connection between paranormal myth and penis splitting becomes quite clear. It is far more reasonable to suspect that certain paranormal beliefs *preceded* penis splitting than to suggest that penis splitting was a useful cultural adaptation to specific environmental conditions.

This is just one of an endless array of examples that would lead us to the conclusion that culture does not *cause* or produce paranormal beliefs as such. Rather, culture is a human invention that accommodates the universal paranormal belief imperative. Religion, and especially organized religion, happens to be the best that culture can do with our inherent quest for illusion. Culture determines the specific beliefs and rituals that will be maintained in order to satisfy our need to restructure our perceptions of the world. But we are *born* "religious" and suggestible. We wait hungrily for culture to keep us pacified and mesmerized with reality-masking beliefs.

All paranormal believing comes back to the problem of intelligence. When we lost the luxury of ignorance somewhere in our evolutionary past, religion and other self-transcending belief systems came into the evolutionary scene. Our species would combat self-awareness and the unknown with counter-intelligent and non-rational methods of construing the world. However, we were still left with the serious problem of how to convert unbelievable nonsense into something believable. Some process at the level of our everyday lives was required to "launder" reality and to make a warped reality seem *normal*. That was exactly the purpose and function of culture. We might return to Otto Rank's question, "On what level of illusion does one live?" Rank realized that the intended "level" of illusion was that set out by culture. Fromm saw that some cultures are better than others at instilling people with the "faith" to ignore and override their rational selves.

Bellow, in *Herzog*, echoes Kierkegaard when he refers to our natural distaste for possibility. In one of his many thought-provoking social analyses, Bellow conceives of the origin of culture (the "social order") as our "common primal crime." He goes on to describe the world of culture as the "thick unconscious cloud, the primitive blood-daze." Although a monster in many ways, we love, want, and need it. Through the eyes of Herzog, Bellow describes what humans want from culture. They want "an imaginary human situation invented by their own genius, one which they believe is the only true and the only human reality." In *Seize the Day*, Bellow makes a distinction between two opposing parts of the human being. One is the "pure soul," the other is the "pretender soul." Our pure soul loves the truth, but it suffers and goes hungry, the purpose being "to keep the whole thing going." In my view that "thing" is the cultural machine. Our pretender soul is under social control. It is "the society mechanism." Bellow calls the pretender soul a "lie." That, he says, is "the main tragedy of human life." He mourns this aspect of our fate through Herzog: "Oh, it is terrible! Terrible! You are not free. Your own betrayer is inside of you and sells you out. You have to obey like a slave."

Ernest Becker's lucid thinking puts light on the important interactions between culture and paranormal belief. He made the observation that "man lives his contradictions, for better or worse, in some kind of cultural project." As a result, we are successfully limited to the "safe dosage of life which is prescribed by culture."[8] Then, according to Becker, "the average man is at least secure that the cultural game *is* the truth, the unshakable, durable truth."[9] Becker, like Fromm, singled out Western culture as the most "spiritually" bankrupt of all known human cultures. The failure of Western culture is the result of the erosion of the all-important *conventional* self-transcending belief systems. A discussion of the existential confusion and the unhealthy proliferation of second-rate paranormal beliefs in Western culture will be reserved for a later chapter dealing with the mental health crisis taking place in this society. For now, let us consider Becker's provocative discourse on culture as it relates to illusion and self-deception.

Becker defined culture quite simply as a "lie," and more precisely a "macro-lie." That is, culture is the source of untruths that serve to take us away from reality and ourselves. In *The Eighth Day*, Thornton Wilder makes a similar point in saying, "it is the duty of the old to lie to the young."[10] These lies serve to strengthen us and help to fend off the despair that always threatens to erode our false learned hopes. We believe the "lies" for the good of ourselves and our species. Culture floods us with the socially sanctioned suggestions that keep us "partially self-hypnotized," as Becker puts it. In addition to feeding our suggestibility in this manner, culture *normalizes* this necessary form of madness. It does so by making the insane beliefs about reality into *majority* beliefs and behavior. Fromm used the term "cultural patterning" to describe this procedure by which the majority can come to perceive their own *absolute* insanity as normality. Once most people are doing or believing something, it no longer matters how crazy it is. In fact, once this normalizing of behavior has taken place, true sanity is usually seen as insane since it falls outside the boundaries of culture's patterning.

The fact that culture is able to normalize absolutely insane people and beliefs is of utmost importance. If a culture is functioning optimally, it should create a "bar to the exercise of free rationality," as La Barre notes.[11] With that accomplished, members of a culture can become immersed with almost any degree of reality distortion. While relying on our ever-ready suggestibility, culture molds our perceptual worlds with suggestions that are hopefully digestible by the mass of people. As lifelong hypnotic subjects of culture, we are usually able to feel normal in our reality distortion and absolute insanity.

One can quite easily interchange the words "normal" and "culture." In *Equus*, Peter Shaffer describes "normal" in precisely the same way I am trying to depict culture. The passage is powerful and reflects not only the nature of the beast we are calling "normal," but the bitter-sweet effect it has on us: "Normal is the good smile in a child's eye – and also the dead stare in a million adults. It both sustains and kills like a god. Normal is the indispensable murderous god of health."[12]

A sense is conveyed that "normal," or culture, is both an asset and a liability. It is a reassured child, but also the half-awake and half-alive one who is fed on illusion and fabrication. In being made into "normal" cogs of culture, we are sustained and deadened at the same time. Culture gives us necessary refuge from reality and ourselves but that same sanctuary is also a prison. Culture, like "normal," is an indispensable god. In that way, it is a god of health and, in particular, mental health. Culture is also a murderous god, however, as it claims the fee of our rationality and personal freedom. Culture makes morons, albeit confident and healthy morons, of all of us. The label "murderous god of health" captures all the essential features of culture as the macro-force that dominates our mental processes. Shaffer's description of this good killer god and its effect on us reveals the fundamentally contradictory manner in which the human animal is destined to live. We are under the hypnotic command of culture and its suggestions. These pattern our conscious and unconscious perceptions of the world into "normal" untruths and misperceptions of reality.

In speaking of "normal," one is also speaking of conformity. Culture relies on our naturally occurring suggestibility in order to make people's perceptions and beliefs conform to one another. Without suggestibility, it is unlikely that conformity of belief would have been possible. The "macro-lie" could be threatened. Morris Shames of Canada's Concordia University actually studied the relationship between conformity and suggestibility.[13] In line with the above reasoning, he found a strong positive correlation between the extent of conformity and the degree of suggestibility in the people studied. Therefore, conformity seems to be one feature of the murderous god Normal, or Culture.

Rank wrote that "the essence of normality is the *refusal of reality*."[14] In arriving at that conclusion, Rank was describing the "priority of the irrational life force" within each of us. This irrational life-force is nothing more than what we have been calling our appetite for paranormal, self-transcending belief. It is culture that *steers* our suggestibility and our drive for the irrational. Becker makes reference to our "willing slavishness" to the pre-set belief systems that make up culture. He comments on how easy it is for the average person to be made "automatic, predictable, and pathetic" by giving in so readily to this craving for "the spell." It is again a *cultural* spell that we are under.

Paul Schilder, the well-known psychoanalyst, also speaks of the everyday hypnotic trance that characterizes all groups of people. Schilder mourns our inevitable submission to the "spell" because he feels that, at some level, we see in that act of submission our own timidity and cowardice. In that respect, he also comments that the everyday hypnotic trance lacks the dignity of many other wholehearted passions.[15] On that point, I am inclined to disagree somewhat with Schilder. True, we sometimes encounter slight reservations when giving over ourselves to beliefs about a modified reality. But I believe that such temporary misgivings are only experienced by people who are in a defective culture and being offered ruptured and only partially effective belief systems. This, as we shall see, is a relatively common occurrence in Western culture.

The view that culture functions as a psychological defense mechanism is not a new one. In *Culture, the Human Plan*, Charles Case writes that, fundamentally, "culture is an attempt to order the chaos of existence."[16] Case explains that, in order to transform chaos into order, culture must "make people act in similar ways and . . . create *recognizable* collective behavior."[17]

In *The Sacred Canopy*, Peter Berger writes similarly that "the social world arises from the externalization of human consciousness to construct a world of roles, rules . . . and beliefs."[18] This also suggests a need on the part of the individual to abandon personal consciousness in favor of a mass consciousness based in culture. In that same work, Berger states that culture is, in fact, "the product of *patterned* consciousness." Therefore, the reality of the human condition cannot be convincingly disguised or altered on an individual basis.

Culture is what delivers and coordinates the belief systems that protect us. Even though we believers are defended by our beliefs, it is none the less accurate to envision culture as the all-encompassing *defense mechanism* from which all our individual defenses originate. To act out our paranormal belief imperatives in the absence of culture would be an invitation for further chaos. To manufacture reality-transcending beliefs in isolation from one another would result in total social confusion.

Most importantly, the vital self-transcending beliefs offered by any one culture must have *consensual validation*. That term, originally coined by Fromm, means that a belief is accepted as fundamentally true by a large section of society. Fromm saw that it was necessary for "insane" ideas and beliefs to be consensually validated before they could create the foundation for the absolute insanity of an entire culture. Once the populace gives its collective stamp of approval to a belief (in this case, a paranormal belief), it is more likely to be effective in establishing a protective shelter from reality. If that is accomplished, the natural suggestibility of the people in that culture becomes absorbed into a *limited* set of beliefs. They will achieve their necessary "everyday trance" and thus be enabled to function "normally" in their half-awake hypnotic state. Normal insanity will have been produced and the "murderous god of health" will have done its job. All is well (or as well as it can be for us) under those conditions. And we remain generally isolated from other groups and subgroups with competing and incompatible belief systems. Ideally, the amount of destruction we impart to those with differing paranormal beliefs is small in relation to the benefits obtained from the beliefs themselves. When all goes according to the grand evolutionary plan, we become the "genius earthworm" and the "glorious refuse of the universe," of which Pascal wrote.

## Good cultures and bad cultures

It does not matter in the least whether the paranormal beliefs we hold are true or not. From the reasoning that I offer here, it would seem that they are inevitable systems of ignorance that harness the power of "pure intelligence." If belief in all our paranormal nonsense were a product of choice, one might be more inclined to don the existential dunce's cap. But it is not. We owe our very existence to our ability to filter and re-shape our perceptions of the world. Not only that, we should recognize that our beliefs *must* be bizarre and in total defiance of reason and logic. Pascal said exactly this in referring to religious paranormal beliefs and practices. In *Pensées*, he wrote that religious beliefs *must* contradict nature, common sense, and even pleasure. This fact makes it even more important that paranormal beliefs should also be *unverifiably* false; that is, that they cannot be shown to be false. The fact that they cannot be proven true is of no consequence. What we have come to call "faith" will prevail even in the complete absence of evidence that something is true.

Our innermost drive to find reality-transcending belief systems is so strong that it can temporarily withstand proof that the beliefs are false. In *The True Believer,* Hoffer echoes Bergson's words in stating that the "strength of faith . . . manifests itself not in moving mountains but in *not* seeing mountains to move."[19] That is still another way of saying that we thrive on healthy stupidity and healthy blindness. None the less, evidence suggests that, in the short term, we have the amazing ability to cling to blatantly false beliefs even after they are exposed as false. Even more spectacularly, our belief in any false belief is temporarily *enhanced* by the negative evidence. That finding is support for the idea that we do, in fact, employ the defenses that I proposed earlier. These guard against what are hopefully only occasional and infrequent revelations that we have swallowed a mental placebo. Yet even our tenacious drives to ignore the truth about the moving mountains was not designed to withstand constant testing of our reality-transcending beliefs. In the face of verifiable contrary evidence, our "canopy of belief" will start to develop psychic "leaks," which threaten our beliefs as well as our mental health. Then, we must spend more valuable energy on the arduous mental task of finding new sets of beliefs with which to shelter ourselves.

The disciples of doomsday leaders serve to illustrate this point. A number of social psychologists have studied various doomsday prophets and their followers. Invariably, the doomsday leader espoused the message that, at a certain specified time, the world would end. God would appear and judge his or her people. (Other animals usually get left out of the picture.) Those prepared for Judgment Day would sally forth with God into the sky for an eternity of pampered bliss. The disciples were ready and waiting when the day came. In each case, the world did not end. The sun kept rising and all of nature continued to eat itself, just as it has done since the dawn of life on this planet. The social psychologists were especially interested in what happened to the disciples' faith in the leader whose convincing words were proven wrong. Keep in mind that a great many followers gave up all their earthly possessions in preparation for the wonderful end. To their amazement, researchers found that the faith of the disciples actually *increased* after the world failed to end. A simple rationalization on the part of the leader was sufficient to restore and even bolster belief. In his fine article *Making Sense of the Nonsensical*, Neal Osherow writes about this rationalization process and how it led over 900 people at Jonestown to kill themselves for someone preaching what should have been recognized as utter nonsense.[20]

There is a serious problem, however, with paranormal beliefs that can be tested or checked as to their validity. Although rationalization will conquer fact and uphold paranormal fictions for short spans of time, *verifiably* false belief systems tend to crumble and become displaced over longer periods. If available, people will gravitate toward unverifiable beliefs. It is the most important function of any culture to provide people with believable beliefs. These beliefs should be sufficiently vague and non-specific so as to withstand critical analysis. If a culture fails at this principal task, we must conclude that the culture is basically flawed.

Some colleagues and I were aware that Japan is unique in that the Japanese people have relatively little belief in a god or traditional religion generally. Similar surveys in India and the United States (two of the most religious countries in the world) show that percentage to be as high as 95 percent while those conducted in Australia have those percentages slightly lower (50–85 percent depending on the survey). The most recent survey on religious belief in Australia was conducted by a group of researchers at the National University in Canberra. It found that 88 percent of people maintained belief in some sort of god. That was a slight increase from surveys conducted in earlier years.

In Japan, however, the largest survey showed that less than 20 percent held religious beliefs, and only 14 percent described religious beliefs as "very important" to them.[21] Eighteen percent reported belief in life after death, a fraction of the percentage of Australians holding that belief. These findings prompted us to hypothesize that the Japanese would be more vulnerable to death anxiety than an Australian comparison group. (An Australian comparison group was used for convenience purposes as I was living and teaching in Australia at the time.) Thanks to my Japanese research assistant Satoko Kawahara and two Japanese academics who helped with survey translations, we were able to embark on an ambitious cross-cultural study of death anxiety in Japan and Australia. The results were in the predicted direction, with Japanese subjects having much higher death anxiety levels.

The higher death anxiety on the part of the Japanese may have to do with insufficient *quantity* or degree of paranormal belief offered by their culture. There is always a psychological cost to members of a society where cultural "lies" are less available or less developed. The Japanese are a prime example, as they are consistently found to have the greatest prevalence of neurotic symptoms of any major culture so far studied by cross-cultural psychologists. They have the highest levels of anxiety and depression. Some studies have involved the administration of the MMPI (Minnesota Multiphasic Personality Inventory) to people in various cultures. That is the most widely used personality test used by Western psychologists. When this 566-item test is given to groups of people from various cultures, the Japanese show marked elevations on several of the ten scales designed to measure mental disturbance.

One might argue that this is a product of translation problems into the Japanese language. Yet the findings are too consistent and too many in number to be ignored on that basis. I believe that the greater neuroticism observed in the Japanese can be largely understood in terms of the sparsity of unverifiably false paranormal beliefs. As a society of people, they do not seem to compensate fully for this weak cultural illusion system and they pay a price in terms of mental health. This is not necessarily bad. In fact, the reverse may be true. The mental health penalty may be a small price to pay for some degree of freedom from paranormal self-deception. This point should come clear shortly when we consider the horrific destructiveness that derives from our need to escape reality via self-transcending belief systems.

Western culture has severe problems of its own. Something seems to have robbed us of our cheer. An unsettling number of great thinkers have depicted us as extremely dreary and unsatisfied people. This is all the more ironic given the wealth and physical comfort that the majority of us enjoy. Personally, I have found it a challenge to explain the consistency with which some of our best minds portray us as such miserable creatures. Albert Schweitzer viewed Westerners as incomplete and poorly integrated people who were dependent and passive to a pathological degree. Einstein held the view that Western man is suffering from a process of deterioration and that we are crippled with insecurity and loneliness to the extent that we are incapable of enjoying life. In *Beyond Psychology*, Rank speaks of "utter despair of modern man." Fromm comments that "we are a society of notoriously unhappy, lonely, anxious, depressed, destructive and dependent people who are glad when we have killed the time we are trying to save."[22]

The authors of these criticisms undoubtedly differed in their explanations for our apparently dismal state. Yet, one has to wonder what it is about Western culture that has left us in such terrible spiritual and psychological shape. While few mental health professionals would disagree that Western culture is in the grips of a mental health crisis and an upsurge in social problems, the cause of this situation remains unclear. However, in *The Moral Order*, the anthropologist Raoul Naroll explains how some cultures are far more effective than others at safeguarding the mental health of its members. Naroll introduces the concept of the "moral net." This "net" is the network of customs, beliefs, and related practices that manufacture "knowledge" and "understanding" of the world. In turn, they establish a framework around which morality and acceptable pro-social behavior is built. The moral net, according to Naroll, defines the "correct" way by which we should live and make sense of the world. It channels and utilizes the suggestibility of its members in a maximally efficient manner.

Of course, religious and other paranormal myths make up a large part of this safety net. In some cultures, this moral net is relatively intact. In others, certain factors have torn away at its fabric and caused confusion, disorientation, and a host of social ills and psychological problems. Western culture has a horribly tattered moral net. In particular, the belief systems that once allowed us to invent believable "knowledge" about the world are all but useless in holding back reality. This is despite the apparent resurgence of various types of paranormal beliefs, including religious ones, that have been witnessed in recent years.

In *The Sane Society*, Fromm explains that Western culture is a very "bad" one and, as a consequence, existential anxiety has reached epidemic proportions. His theoretical view, known as humanistic sociopsychoanalysis, considers myth-making and self-transcendence to be essential requisites to mental health. However, it is not the job of the individual to manufacture these belief systems, according to Fromm. He states that myths must be *conventional*, something that can only be accomplished by culture. Peace, harmony, and mental health will reign if our myths are conventional and in common usage. In the preface to *Our Town*, Thornton Wilder gives a good definition of the word "convention" as it is being used here. He calls a convention "an agreed-upon falsehood, an *accepted* untruth." If our beliefs were not generally accepted and agreed-upon, we would feel self-conscious and foolish. That by itself would tarnish our priceless illusions.

This crucial point is illustrated by a charming interview with a twelve-year-old girl whom David Riesman mentions in *The Lonely Crowd*.[23]

> Girl: I like Superman better than the others because they can't do anything Superman can do. Batman can't fly and that is important.
> Interviewer: Would you like to be able to fly?
> Girl: I would like to be able to fly if everyone else did, but otherwise it would be kind of conspicuous.

The girl was right. Superman is preferable to Batman. The more fantastic and removed from reality our beliefs are, the better we fare psychologically. They should be as absolutely insane as possible. With regard to paranormal self-deception, jumbo-sized lies work better than small and verifiable ones. However, the belief in big lies depends on culture patterning those beliefs into mass consciousness. Like the young girl, we all have a basic desire to fly – a desire to fly above reality. Evolution gave us the wings to ride our illusions to dizzying heights. But we can only do that if a large portion of our culture is aboard those illusions. Otherwise, our beliefs are impotent against what lingers on the lips of that damned idiot we know as life, as truth.

It happens that Western culture is floundering at its paramount task of making its myths generally acceptable and, therefore, inconspicuous. In the final chapter, we shall examine the present state of Western paranormal beliefs. We shall see that the current incompetence of Western culture has led many of our established illusions to become transparent. In a sense, what we see are lots of flightless Batmen trying unsuccessfully to take the place of a dying Superman.

It is now time to take an objective look at the relative advantages and disadvantages of the paranormal belief adaptation. In the following chapter, I shall attempt to do this by drawing on a wide range of psychological research dealing directly and indirectly with belief in the paranormal. At the same time, I shall try to avoid the jungle of technical terms that makes psychological research reports seem so heartless and unintelligible.

# 5 *Paranormal Belief: Our Cruel Savior*

It is sometimes quite easy to see both the advantages and disadvantges that are associated with a particular paranormal belief. For example, numerous groups in South-East Asia and the Western Pacific have "cargo cult" beliefs. They believe that a large ship loaded with all sorts of goods will soon magically arrive on their shores. In a study of these belief systems, Peter Worsley writes about the manner in which these beliefs increase people's overall level of happiness and personal security.[1] At the same time, however, these beliefs are maladaptive because they lower motivation to work and *independently* to resolve their economic problems. Another example might be the Roman Catholics who believe that they are pleasing a god by refraining from the use of birth control. That belief, as part of their larger network of religious beliefs, undoubtedly affords the believer a sense of order, direction, and meaning that is good for that person. The bad side of that belief is the matter of overpopulation which presents problems on both small and global levels. Even so, the advantages of such beliefs probably outweigh the disadvantages.

Paranormal belief, as an evolutionary tactic, appears to be a mixed psychological blessing. That is true of many, or most evolutionary strategies. Even so, if they do actually limit the emotional damage that would stem from "pure intelligence" alone, we should acknowledge that they have historically afforded more benefits than liabilities. There is no doubt that we have come to thrive as a species, and we undoubtedly owe credit to our ability to keep reality at bay with self-transcending beliefs. However, adaptations often outlive their usefulness. This may well be the case with the adaptation that enabled paranormal belief. In fact, the very adaptation that enabled us to survive the impact that reality had on consciousness may be what spells the end of our extraordinary species. But before we reflect on what may prove to be the steepest cost of the paranormal belief adaptation, let us weigh up the relative benefits and costs of paranormal believing as they can now be tallied. Such a discussion can be placed in the context of Tolstoy's insight from the 1890 work *Kreuzer Sonata* that both our salvation and our punishment lie in our ability to befog ourselves. The word "befog" is synonymous with "deceive" in that statement. And we shall see that paranormal self-transcendence does both psychologically save and punish us.

## Paranormal salvation

### Mental health advantages

Taken as a whole, available research shows that paranormal beliefs are psychologically good for us if they are *conventional* in nature. By this, I mean they are good for our mental health. Traditional religious paranormal beliefs seem to be the "best" paranormal beliefs to have in this respect. They are far more likely to be unverifiably false and to be sanctioned by a large percentage of the population. Paranormal believing does not appear to be as mentally beneficial if the beliefs fall outside of mainstream cultural ideology.

With a few exceptions, research shows that people who hold religious paranormal beliefs are generally happier and more satisfied with their lives.[2] Some of these studies involved simple ratings of overall happiness and contentment, while others used standardized questionnaires about general life-satisfaction. Several investigators have found that people with strong religious paranormal beliefs are less inclined to suffer from psychological disturbance and general emotional distress. Keeping in mind the rough distinction between neurotic and psychotic disorders, we find that paranormal believing safeguards people from neurotic forms of mental disturbance. Specifically, they protect people from disorders with compulsive, ruminative, and highly ritualized symptoms. This should not be surprising, given that most religions foster healthy versions of these same types of "symptoms." Schizophrenia and related disorders are no more prevalent in non-believers than believers. We now know that these are biochemical diseases and, as such, have only a small psychological component. Parenthetically, however, it is quite interesting that extreme religiosity is frequently a symptom of paranoid schizophrenia. Fanatical religious beliefs probably represent a direct response to the schizophrenia symptoms. They may help to combat the frightening chaos that characterizes the mental world of victims of that unfortunate illness.

David Hay and Margaret Morisy compared the mental status of people who had mystical-religious experiences to those who did not.[3] They defined such experience as "an awareness of a presence which is not perceptible to the ordinary organs of sense." These often involved a spontaneous "quasi-perception" of something sacred, such as God, an angel, a saint, or a "force" of supernatural origin. Hay and Morisy carried out tests of mental health on people who reported mystical-religious experiences. They administered the same tests to those who did not have such experiences. They found that people who have mystical-religious experiences are emotionally and psychologically *better* adjusted than those who do not have such experiences.

Suicide rates are consistently lower among people with religious paranormal beliefs than their non-religious counterparts.[4] There are several types of suicide, and each form has slightly different predisposing factors. None the less, approximately 80 percent of suicides are preceded by severe depression. Since traditional paranormal beliefs reduce one's chances of suffering from depression, we would expect lower suicide rates in people with these beliefs. More specifically, orthodox religious beliefs seem to reduce the incidence of certain types of suicide. One category of suicide has been termed "existential." That is the form of suicide to which Camus referred in *The Myth of Sisyphus*.[5] In the opening lines of that book, he states that the only important question we have to ask ourselves is whether or not we should kill ourselves. Some of us are prone to contemplate what Camus calls "the burden of enduring hypocrisy" and the overall meaninglessness and purposelessness of life. The person who commits existential suicide has lost the motivation to continue existing. Benjamin Franklin was speaking figuratively when he wrote in a 1749 issue of *Poor Richard's Almanac* that "nine in ten men are suicides." However, nine in ten of us might be literal suicides if we did not have the beliefs to disguise the Void, and to find motivation in healthy fictions about our conditions. Conventional reality-defying beliefs do that for most of us.

All that has been said to this point would lead us to predict that traditional religious paranormal beliefs have important prophylactic properties in terms of mental health. Earlier, I made the statement that *absolute* insanity, in the form of socially sanctioned paranormal belief, protects us from *clinical* insanity. That is precisely why, with some inevitable exceptions, experimental studies reveal that those with traditional religious beliefs fare better on measures of mental health. Freud makes this point quite explicitly when he writes in *The Future of an Illusion*: "the true believer is in a high degree protected against the danger of neurotic afflictions; by accepting the *universal* neurosis he is spared the task of forming a personal neurosis."[6]

Again we come back to the basic premise that one type of insanity spares us another, more painful encounter with insanity. Of course, the "healthy" insane person is, in Freud's words, the true believer, the one who can effectively distort reality. Ernest Becker also speaks of neurosis as a problem of reality versus illusion. Since in his formulation the *reality* of the human condition is too much for us, the psychologically healthy person is the one who can achieve an optimal level of illusion and self-deception. These come most effectively in the form of established conventional belief systems.

I have conducted and published some research that compared the mental health of atheists to a group of individuals with strong traditional religious beliefs.[7] I gave subjects a detailed mental health questionnaire, as well as Tobacyk's Paranormal Belief Scale.[8] That particular measure of paranormal belief provides an overall score indicating one's degree of belief in the paranormal. In addition, it gives a score on seven separate subscales that measure belief in specific aspects of the paranormal. These are: Traditional Religion, Psi, Witchcraft, Superstition, Spiritualism, Extraordinary Life Forms, and Precognition.

I found that people with traditional religious beliefs had significantly fewer symptoms of mental illness than the atheists. That supported my theory that people have a need for a fixed amount of paranormal beliefs. If they fall short, they suffer psychological consequences. So, maybe there is truth to what

Camus said in *The Myth of Sisyphus,* namely that once we fall prey to truths we cannot free ourselves from them. It seems to be the case that once a "lie" is lost, it is lost forever. It may be that some rare unfortunates never find these cultural fibs. In either case, the price is neurosis and/or diminished life enjoyment.

In that study, I also tested a theory of mine which I labeled "Belief Deficit Compensation." It is also based on the idea that all of us require a certain quantity of reality-defying belief. In addition, however, I reasoned that it does not matter so much what *type* of paranormal belief one uses to irrationally disguise, alter, or expand reality. That led me to hypothesize that we can *compensate* for a deficit in one area of paranormal belief by increasing belief in other areas. This meant that I was expecting the atheists (with no traditional religious paranormal beliefs) to compensate for that deficit by believing more in the things contained on the six other subscales. I was wrong in that prediction. People with traditional religious paranormal beliefs were actually somewhat *more* likely to have other types of paranormal beliefs. Conversely, the atheists were *less* likely to hold other forms of paranormal belief. I was forced to conclude that those with low levels of paranormal belief do not compensate with other paranormal beliefs, and that they pay a mental health price for failing to do so. I have since found other work showing that people with one type of paranormal belief are more likely to have other paranormal beliefs.[9] Another thing I learned from that study was how very few people there are that have *no* paranormal beliefs. Of the hundreds of people surveyed, the number with no paranormal belief whatsoever could be counted on the fingers of one hand!

It seems that socially sanctioned religious paranormal beliefs are simply *better* at protecting our psychological and emotional health than ones that do not enjoy acceptance by the majority. That alone can account for much of the mental health difference found between those with traditional as compared to non-traditional paranormal beliefs. Additional evidence of the psychological benefits of conventional paranormal believing comes from research focused on specific emotions, such as anxiety, death anxiety, and depression. Some research has examined the effects of "approved" religious paranormal beliefs on anxiety levels. Strong religious beliefs are typically associated with lower levels of stress and anxiety.[10] Correlational studies usually report an inverse correlation between religiosity and anxiety. That is, the more one adheres to traditional religious paranormal belief and ritual, the *lower* is one's anxiety.

In one interesting study, interviews were carried out with soldiers who had been in active combat situations. It was found that 75 percent of those men resorted to prayer in an effort to control their fear and anxiety. That same study also found that those with the highest stress and anxiety levels were the most likely to turn to prayer. Another study measured anxiety levels of those who had just undergone sudden religious conversion.[11] They were much *higher* than the general population, suggesting that dramatic shifts to religious paranormal belief systems can be motivated by excessive anxiety. Over time, one would expect these beliefs to have a stabilizing effect on such inordinately high levels of anxiety. In fact, case histories abound with people who come to find indescribable peace and oceanic bliss once the conversion gives order to their anxious and unordered lives. Undoubtedly, part of this stems from the fact that such individuals are enjoying their own brain endorphins. Who would ever want to give that up just to be brought down to reality?

Death anxiety is one specific type of anxiety that appears to be effectively reduced through traditional religious paranormal beliefs. Paranormal beliefs *should* reduce death anxiety if, in fact, our affinity for such believing evolved so we could distance ourselves from that and other unsavory realities. A number of studies have reported clear *inverse* relationships between fear of death and belief in traditional religious dogma.[12] The more one is able to maintain such religious beliefs, the less anxiety about death one encounters.

Further support for the ability of religious paranormal beliefs to fend off death anxiety comes from a number of studies that examine religious belief as a function of age. It is safe to say that people become more aware of death as they approach old age. It follows that, at some level, people would experience some related anxiety at the prospect of personal oblivion. If religious beliefs act to quell the anxiety associated with the reality of mortality, people should turn to religious beliefs as they get older. In a research review on religiosity and the ageing process, R. G. Kuhlen summarizes the findings on this subject as follows: "in all studies examined, with the exception of those related to church attendance, trends indicate an *increased* interest in and concern about religion as age increases, even into extreme old age."[13]

There is little doubt that many people embrace religious

paranormal beliefs to ward off fear and anxiety stemming from the encroaching reality of death. It is somewhat puzzling why people tend to *disengage* themselves from actual church attendance as they progress in age. It could have to do with some of the problems aged people have in getting themselves physically to a church. Or, it could be a reflection of a different, more personal type of relationship these people have to their revitalized religious beliefs.

Some systems of organized paranormal belief work better than others. For example, cross-cultural studies of religion and death anxiety show that *quality* of religious belief varies from one culture to another, as judged by the ability of those beliefs to control death anxiety. Elizabeth Kubler-Ross wrote that "Eastern" religions are some of the best at controlling fear of death.[14] Alida Westman and Francis Canter actually compared death anxiety levels in those with Eastern and Western types of religious paranormal beliefs.[15] Their results demonstrate that people with Eastern religious beliefs have significantly *less* fear of death than those endorsing Western, primarily Christian, beliefs. Westman and Canter explain their interesting findings in terms of the way in which Eastern religions tend to view death as "an incident of ongoing existence," as well as their belief that the best way to conquer death is to view life and death as inseparable aspects of reality. This they contrast with the more "materialistic" (in the philosophical sense) Western religious belief systems that typically equate death of body with the death of one's personal self.

I tested this with some colleagues by comparing death anxiety levels in a group of Malaysian and Australian people.[16] Hinduism and Buddhism were the primary religions of the Malaysian subjects, whereas all of the Australians had traditional Christian religious beliefs. We realized that a number of other factors could produce varying death anxiety levels between cultures. These might include different methods of child-rearing, the fact that Westerners tend to "hide" death, or even the differing death rates that occur across cultures. Some or all of these could have affected our results, but the *direction* that these would have influenced death anxiety was, and remains, unclear. We felt that the primary conventional belief systems would have an overriding effect on death anxiety. Therefore, we predicted that Western subjects would have signficantly greater fear of death than our Eastern subjects. That is what we found. While this is further support for the concept that belief systems vary in *quality*, another possible explanation should be considered. This concerns the *intactness* of beliefs, in this case traditional religious beliefs. Quite a few social philosophers have commented that, despite surface appearance, Western religion is losing its credibility. If traditional religious beliefs serve to regulate fear of death, the elevated death anxiety in Westerners may reflect a weakness in their conventional belief systems. I suspect this is the case.

The advantages of non-religious paranormal beliefs are not as obvious as with beliefs couched in mainstream religion. Research on the personality and mental health correlates of these beliefs shows conflicting findings. One study by Stuart and Lucille Blum did find that superstitious beliefs were therapeutic in that they served to reduce anxiety and to increase people's sense of control.[17] That study revealed an amazing variety and degree of superstitious paranormal belief in the general population. They reported on the 24 most prevalent superstitious beliefs. Nearly 30 percent of people surveyed reported at least some belief that walking under a ladder would cause events in their life to deteriorate. More than 17 percent of respondents said that walking under a ladder would exert a "strong influence" on events. Similar percentages of people believed that their lives would be affected if mirrors were broken, umbrellas were opened indoors, or black cats crossed their paths. Over 25 percent of those in the survey believed that they could get positive control over life-events by knocking on wood, crossing their fingers, and securing a four-leaf clover. Blum and Blum make the noteworthy observation that superstitious beliefs are more likely to be relied upon in cultures where order, or even the myth of order, are being undermined. Other thinkers on this subject would agree that superstitious beliefs can function to eliminate uncertainty and to give the illusion of control and predictability in one's life.[18]

In direct contrast to the above findings, several other researchers have found that certain non-religious paranormal beliefs are actually a psychological liability to people. Tobacyck's research showed that belief in superstition, witchcraft, and spiritualism was associated with *higher* levels of death anxiety. Other studies have found that these and other non-religious paranormal beliefs were correlated with emotional and psychological maladjustment.[19] Still other experimental work has been unable to determine if non-religious beliefs are harmful or beneficial with regard to certain measures of mental health and general well-being.[20] Therefore, at this point, the available evidence is too confusing to make definitive conclusions about the relative merits of non-religious paranormal beliefs. It is possible that future research will find that some types of non-religious beliefs are psychologically beneficial, while others are detrimental. One conclusion that seems warranted from what we know is that non-religious beliefs do not work as well as religious ones.

Another reason for the apparent reduced effectiveness of non-religious beliefs may be the potential falsifiability of the less sophisticated and less developed non-religious paranormal beliefs. While "good" paranormal beliefs are not able to be proven false, many non-religious paranormal beliefs lack the built-in rationalizations and self-forgiving excuses that make them resistant to rational rejection. If, for example, I opt for the belief that a specific earthling has *demonstrable* supernatural capabilities, I am asking for trouble. I might claim that someone has psychokinetic abilities and that this person can make a cardboard box move. In actual fact, someone once made this exact claim to me some time ago, saying they had come into contact with an individual who could make a cardboard box suspended from a string spin. Naturally, I very much wanted to witness this myself, so I pleaded for a demonstration to be arranged. It took great pressure on my part, as the paranormally gifted person in question kept having other things he needed to do. Finally, a demonstration was set up and I even provided a nice box from the local grocer. Needless to say, the cardboard box hung there like all good boxes do when suspended from a string in a room without a strong draft. The one with the supernatural power resembled a severely constipated person working toward relief as he tried in vain to influence the box.

Since that time, I have witnessed countless failures of paranormal abilities, so many in fact that I once thought that maybe *I* had a unique paranormal ability. Since no one could ever display any paranormal powers in my presence, I wondered if I had the power to *stop* paranormal power in others! When I was not present, people could supposedly perform. When I was there with my nose close to the scene, their powers disappeared. Somehow that fleeting theory never took hold and I quickly snuggled back into my left brain with the conviction that, in all likelihood, everything operates *normally*.

The belief in psychokinesis is a "bad" paranormal belief. So is belief in ESP, clairvoyance, crystals, astrology, numerology, psychic channeling, precognition, palmistry, I Ching, tarot readings, pyramidology, all types of divination, and many other non-religious paranormal phenomena. They are too vulnerable to falsification. If you look closely enough, long enough, and critically enough, they become exposed. (That is why parapsychologists usually run like rabbits when a respectable methodologically-skilled experimenter shows up at their laboratory doors.) As a consequence, closely scrutinized beliefs lose much of their self-deception value. Even worse, they have to withstand suspicion that is automatically roused by beliefs that fall outside of convention. They are already too weak by their very nature and, barring a total collapse of conventional belief, stand little chance of *working* for the believer.

This is not to say that an upsurge of these beliefs cannot be seen when traditional belief systems become eroded. We know that does happen and we are in one of those times now. But that does not change the fact that these beliefs are "second-rate" beliefs which do not compare in effectiveness to conventional religious beliefs. This is also not to say that some religious beliefs are not better than others. We already saw that to be the case. While religious beliefs are *necessarily* nonsensical and irrational, they should not be highly specific or excessively self-contradictory. People run the risk of being unable to constrain their critical thinking capacities. That places them in danger of being stirred from their waking hypnosis. If that happens, changes and shifts of belief are necessary and that will cause a loss of followers.

I believe the Roman Catholic Church has seen such an eventuation in recent years, something that has led to declining membership. Catholics have been shown to suffer more mental illness than any other denomination of Christianity. Most of these are symptoms and disorders related to anxiety and guilt. In *The Open and Closed Mind*, Milton Rokeach explains this in terms of the extreme rigidity and dogmatism that characterizes Catholic beliefs.[21] Catholicism could well learn from astrology which is widespread and growing in popularity. Astrology, too, is a "bad" belief system. But astrologers know that people will not think if you do not give them anything to think about. In a state of thoughtlessness, people will believe. Astrological messages rely on extreme generalization. They are general to the extent that they could be regarded as "true" by any man, woman, child, or chimpanzee. What is more, much of astrology is good news. The Catholic Church would do well to become *less specific* in its nonsense about the way things are or should be. A bit more cheer would not hurt either. That would lead to greater flexibility and fewer accusations of rigidity and archaism in a fast-changing world.

Future research may delineate more exactly how cognitive self-deception serves us and our dangerously well-developed rational faculties. Some researchers are using new and innovative approaches to study the nature and advantages of cognitive self-deception. For instance, Lyn Abramson and her colleagues at the University of Wisconsin conducted an award-winning study that examined the effects of self-deception on level of depression. Using an elaborate social psychological research design, they categorized subjects on the basis of how much "illusion of control" they perceived themselves to have over the experimental conditions. In actuality, it was an empirical test of the old saying that people are happier if they can see life through rose-colored glasses. They found, in line with that saying, that people who are better at deceiving themselves are less depressed than those who are less adept at creating illusions.[22] The self-deceptions that insulate people from depression were labeled "self-serving cognitive biases" since they enable people to perceive life-events with a "rosy glow," as they put it. Although these investigators did not speculate about the specific mental mechanisms by which we are able to favorably "bias" reality, it provides still further evidence for potential psychological benefits associated with cognitive self-deception.

Paranormal beliefs are the most effective and common means by which we achieve "self-serving" biases in our perception of the world. In that respect, paranormal believing has been our salvation. Unfortunately, a certain price had to be paid for the miracle of paranormal belief. The double-edged nature of para-normal belief is well described by C. Daniel Batson. In referring specifically to the intrinsic orientation toward religious paranormal beliefs, he credits them with helping to free us from the existential concerns that we have already discussed. In contrast, he also speaks of the *bondage* in which these beliefs hold us.[23] The cost exacted by our bondage to belief takes a number of forms. It is worth considering some research and theory related to the growing price tag on the unique capacity of our species to deny its nothingness.[24]

## Paranormal belief as our punishment

We can assume that, until now, paranormal believing carried more advantages than disadvantages. I say "until now" because we have reached an evolutionary stage in which reality distortion is becoming a counterproductive adaptation. That is, we may have arrived at what Dobzhansky called an "evolutionary dead end." But before we explore the reasoning behind that sobering note, let us describe some of the relatively minor costs of paranormal belief.

### We are cosmic fools

It would not take long to arrive at an existential crisis if one thought seriously about our timid relationship with reality. Our natural drive to flee from the truth makes us into pretenders. We buy refuge from reality at the price of reason. Dostoevsky wrote in *The Underground Man* that we have all become so unused to the *real* world that we cannot even breathe in it. Rilke regrets that most of us are "dead" as a result of "unlived life."[25] I interpret his words to mean that, in becoming so accustomed to an *unreal* life, we get little chance to experience the world as it *really* is. Such thinking resembles that of Kierkegaard who said our primary mission was to conquer freedom and possibility. What sort of victory is that?

When Becker asserted that human beings are only partially alive and "tucked away" in the beyond, he meant that we *necessarily* become deadened with ignorance, illusion, and self-deception.[26] That metaphorical death is part of the price to be paid for our survival, our physical aliveness. We reduce possibility and forfeit freedom as we insulate ourselves with the necessary "ignorance" that accompanies a rejection of reality.

Samuel Butler once described an honest god as the greatest possible achievement of humankind. Yes, gods and all other paranormal self-deceptions are the works of the human being. But, some cosmic masochists like myself might question the nobility of such an accomplishment. Those same pained spirits might even accuse the human animal of more cowardice than nobility. In *Existentialism*, Sartre writes that "god is a useless and costly hypothesis without which everything would be possible."

The gods and other paranormal fictions are by no means useless. A workable god is well worth the price of some human possibility. But one could ask if we do not abandon much of life in the process of defeating possibility. All genuine possibility, as Sartre says, is to be found *in* reality. Are we not made into idiotic, endorphin-addicted fools by our demand for reality distortion? Of course we are! But, being myself a creature of contradiction, let me contradict myself and say we are not fools. We were designed to be foolish. As such, we deserve to be forgiven.

As creatures of illusion, we are forced to play out our lives in a theater of the absurd. Anais Nin made this point perfectly in an article for the *Journal of the Otto Rank Association*.[27] She wrote that "the caricature aspect of life appears whenever the drunkenness of illusion wears off." We are drunk, doped and entranced by illusion and self-deception. If, even for a moment, that wears off, we see ourselves as sad caricatures that act out fictions in a translated world. We are brainwashed prisoners of culture, the main role of which is to program us with pacifying beliefs. Culture is the nipple that sustains us with self-transcending belief, but it is also the absolute enemy of the one who wants to see the world as it is. Culture, as the embodiment of paranormal self-deception, keeps us forever protected from the truth of our condition.

We are so necessarily removed from the truth about the world that it even runs from us when we have made a conscious decision to live with it. The bold spirit may feel a fleeting urge to cut through one layer of fiction, but all that awaits this quixotic adventurer is another layer of cultural fiction that gets mistakened as truth. Very few of us have the will and determination to reject and keep rejecting culture's translated versions of reality. Since it is virtually impossible to escape culture and its belief offerings, our minds cannot achieve absolute knowledge. We become mere extensions of the cultural lie. That might be disturbing to the occasional neurotic who is asking for existential trouble.

*Casualties of the system*

Not everyone is equally adept at embracing culture's assortment of paranormal beliefs. The previously mentioned research demonstrated a considerable variation between people in what we might call *paranormal belief potential*. It was also evident that those with less belief potential paid a price in terms of mental health. These included increased anxiety, depression, and even suicide in some cases. That follows logically, as we would expect them to be less adept at scaring reality away. So, it is possible to speak in terms of casualties that befall the paranormal belief adaptation. It is a minor cost, because a *generally* successful adaptation can afford and absorb some small losses. And, like all adaptations, natural selection must claim the weakest. Our evolutionary history has favored those who were the best paranormal believers. They were more suited for survival and more likely to propagate their genes. Today, some authorities on evolution argue that our species has ceased to evolve *biologically*. They maintain that we now only evolve *culturally*. In either case, it may still be that good paranormal believers are still being selected for survival. One would anticipate that psychologically well-adjusted individuals are more likely to thrive and reproduce over evolutionary time.

Our differing belief potentials help determine the extent to which we adjust to a condition that demands we bypass and override reason, logic, and critical thinking ability. Inefficient believers (i.e., those not as adept at belief) will receive an overdose of reality and are more inclined to suffer from neurosis. That implies insufficient *quantity* of belief. Ineffectual paranormal belief can also indicate that the individual has selected inferior and less potent paranormal beliefs. When our suggestibility becomes derailed in this manner, we end up with "gods" that are not powerful enough to shield us from reality. These "problems of religion" will be the focus of the next chapter.

### Loss of self-awareness

Another cost of our drive to reconstruct reality is a loss of self-awareness. Any form of self-deception involves the withholding of information from oneself. That might be the right hemisphere keeping some types of information from the left. Regardless, paranormal self-deception involves a reduction of *awareness* of certain aspects of the world about us. When we "befog" ourselves, we put at least some of our mental faculties into a "fog." That should be a health-giving fog, one in which we are meant to live.

The research that supports the relationship between paranormal believing and reduced self-awareness is quite interesting. One line of evidence indicates that paranormal believing may have a negative impact on extent of self-knowledge and degree of insight into one's own thoughts and emotions. Such a conclusion derives from research that employs some of the most sophisticated and widely-used personality tests, such as the Minnesota Multiphasic Personality Inventory and the Eysenck Personality Questionnaire. Without explaining the rather involved methods by which such tests are interpreted, I should mention that these tests have a number of scales that measure different dimensions of personality functioning and personality disorders. Some of these scales are called *validity* scales and are a mechanism by which the psychologist can determine if a person is being deceptive. One validity scale on these tests is named the Lie Scale. It usually tells the psychologist if people are, for some conscious or unconscious reason, distorting the accuracy or truthfulness of their responses. High scores on the Lie Scale are also taken as a measure of defensive denial and a lack of self-insight. Such individuals, if not deliberately deceptive, would be regarded as "out of touch" with themselves or their feelings.

With remarkable consistency, people with strong religious paranormal beliefs score much higher than non-religious individuals on these Lie Scales. This should be the case, since defensive denial is at the very heart of our rejection of reality. Such findings have been reported with adult populations and with children as young as eight years. One research team concluded that religious paranormal beliefs actually impede self-awareness.[28] Their rationale was that these, and presumably other, paranormal beliefs require repression and denial of one's emotions, thoughts, and behaviors. All such repression and denial would interfere with self-insight. Leslie Francis and her colleagues also discovered elevated "lie" scores in those with strong religious paranormal beliefs. They agree that this is indicative of diminished self-awareness in those with religious paranormal beliefs. However, they also raise the important chicken-and-egg problem. That is, do religious beliefs *cause* one to lose self-insight and self-awareness, or do people who are already deficient in this respect gravitate toward such beliefs? Francis and her colleagues seem to feel that people who are *already* insightful and self-aware are less inclined to adopt these paranormal beliefs. This is similar to the thinking of Jacques Pohier who viewed religious paranormal believing to be the *result of* cognitive immaturity, or what he called an "infantile mentality."[29] It is also possible that paranormal believing, in and of itself, takes a toll on a person's ability to appraise themselves accurately. One would predict this if paranormal believing is actually an impediment to self-awareness, and also if such belief requires one to bypass one's critical thinking faculties.

A loss of critical thinking ability might be considered another cost of paranormal believing. Research shows, in fact, that paranormal belief affects our capacity to critically analyze our world. In one of the best-designed studies on this topic, James Alcock compared the critical thinking abilities of "believers" and "non-believers" in the paranormal.[30] He used the Critical Thinking Appraisal Inventory which measures "the ability to define and analyze a problem, to judge the validity of the inferences made, and to draw conclusions while recognizing stated and unstated assumptions." The results confirmed that believers in the paranormal have significantly *less* critical thinking ability than people who are generally skeptical of the paranormal. Another related experiment dealt solely with religious paranormal belief. In that study, subjects were classified as either "pro-religious" or "anti-religious." The results revealed that people's critical thinking ability *decreased* in proportion to their degree of religious belief. People opposed to religious paranormal belief were clearly superior in that dimension of our mental operations. In summarizing the research in this area, Alcock is quite clear: "believers in the paranormal tend to be more dogmatic in their beliefs and less skilled at critical thinking than are skeptics."[31]

The paranormal belief adaptation was an evolutionary strategy that *intended* us to be less "critical" and less aware of the world in which we live. It follows that we would be less aware of ourselves in the process. In and of itself, diminished self-awareness is a relatively small price to pay for the luxury of illusion and self-deception. However, we shall see that it plays a part in the most serious flaw with the paranormal belief imperative. That flaw is the inhumanity that goes hand in hand with reality transcendence. In fact, our very existence is now jeopardized.

## The creation of evil

Reality-defying beliefs are potentially deadly and destructive. They have become a lethal activity waiting to claim our species. Such a provocative thesis can be backed up with many studies that indicate a clear connection between paranormal believing and a number of personality characteristics that contribute to destructiveness. L.B. Brown, a noted expert on the psychology of religious beliefs, carried out a review of research related to tolerance of others in people with varying levels of religious paranormal belief. Brown concludes that "it is a well-documented fact that more religious people tend to be *less tolerant* of others."[32] With very few exceptions, research also shows that religious paranormal beliefs cause people to be more *prejudiced* and *bigoted*.[33] Most explanations for these findings refer to cognitive styles that operate in those with these religious paranormal beliefs. Albert Ellis, an internationally-known cognitive psychologist, showed how religious paranormal beliefs are cognitively *incompatible* with tolerance for self and others. In his controversial essay, *The Case against Religion*, he went so far as to claim that "religiosity, to a large degree, is masochism, and both religion and masochism are forms of mental sickness . . . that *must* make you self-depreciating and dehumanized."[34] For Ellis, the acceptance of irrational beliefs causes us to "sabotage" ourselves. Not only do such cognitive systems make us masochistic, but sadistic as well. Once dehumanized with beliefs that do not rest on reason and logic, Ellis says we are incapable of tolerance to others in addition to ourselves. As opposed as that might be to our usual conceptions about religious and related paranormal beliefs, most research supports such a conclusion.

In an attempt to sub-categorize religious faith, Michael Argyle determined that *conventional* religious paranormal beliefs are more likely than "private" religious beliefs to be associated with prejudice, bigotry, and intolerance.[35] Gordon Allport, who also found greater prejudice and intolerance in people with religious beliefs, came to a similar conclusion. He categorized religious beliefs as either "extrinsic" or "intrinsic" in nature. Extrinsic religious belief stems from an indiscriminate selection of those beliefs that are conventional and therefore endorsed by the social majority. Intrinsic religion is more personal and individualized. Such beliefs derive from personal experience and one's unique perceptions of the world. Allport found that those with extrinsic religious paranormal beliefs were more prejudiced and bigoted than those with intrinsic religious beliefs.[36] Allport attempts to account for the prejudice and intolerance that one observes in those with traditional religious beliefs. He theorizes that such beliefs lead to "stereotyped over-generalizations" in which others (with differing beliefs) are not regarded as worthwhile individuals. That is, people become categorized in a black/white and good/

bad fashion on the basis of their beliefs. In analyzing Allport's findings, Joseph Byrnes makes an interesting point about the possible value and function of the actual prejudice that derives from religious paranormal belief:

> Religion is not a value in its own right, because it serves other needs and is a purely utilitarian formation! Now, prejudice, too, is a 'useful' formation; it, too, provides security, comfort, status, and social support. A life that is dependent on extrinsic religion is likely to be dependent on the supports of prejudice, hence the positive correlations between extrinsic religious orientation and intolerance.[37]

Prejudice, like religious paranormal believing, may be "useful," but one cannot help but be alerted to some dangers in this type of adaptation.

In 1985, C. Daniel Batson and colleagues conducted an exhaustive review of research that focused on the relationship between religiosity, prejudice, and intolerance.[38] They isolated 44 studies that dealt with this subject. Of those, 34 found a *positive* correlation between conventional religious paranormal belief/ involvement and prejudice! Eight studies failed to find a correlation in any direction; and only *two* of the 44 studies reported a negative correlation between degree of prejudice and religious belief and practice. (It should be mentioned that those two studies were ones that employed pre-adolescents or adolescents.) Batson and co-workers come to "the very clear, if unsettling conclusion . . . that religion is not associated with increased love and acceptance, but with increased intolerance, prejudice and bigotry."[39] They also found, however, that those with conventional (extrinsic) religious beliefs were more prone to these negative personality attributes than those with more private or intrinsic beliefs.

Still other research has determined that established religious paranormal beliefs are associated with personality characteristics that are the precursors to destructive and cruel behavior. For example, it has been shown that people with strong religious beliefs are *less humanitarian* and *more* likely to *favor harsh forms of punishment* than those less inclined to religious paranormal belief.[40] In another study by Gordon Allport, those with strong religious beliefs were found to be more *racially prejudiced* than people with less religious paranormal belief.[41] Research also shows that religious belief and participation results in greater *intolerance of those with differing political persuasions.*[42] Religious people have also been shown to be more *rejecting of individuals who have differing sexual preferences.*[43] Greater degrees of *authoritarianism* and *ethnocentrism* have also been found among people with strong religious paranormal beliefs.[44]

A recent study by New Zealand psychologist, Hamish Dixon, focused specifically on the social demographics of child abuse. One of the principal findings of his study is that people with strong religious paranormal beliefs are much *more likely to be child abusers.*[45] Dixon admitted that it was ironic that it was those "pillars of society" who were predisposed to this cruel and brutal brand of inhumanity. Still, if culture or society is a "lie" about reality, one would expect the "pillars of society" to be the personification of those lies. They would, in fact, be expected to have the greatest distortions of the world around them. Their distorted perceptions of the world could easily include the way they perceive and react to a child's behavior. A Californian psychologist, Lowell Streiker, also found that people with strong religious paranormal beliefs are more inclined toward child abuse and other forms of *sadistic* behavior.[46]

One is inexorably led to the conclusion that, even though religious paranormal believing is good for us, it is not *entirely* good. Our seemingly heaven-bent believers are hellions at heart. We are tempted to agree with Elizabeth McClaren's conclusion in *The Nature of Belief*: "While in the past it was a tolerable way of coping with anxiety, the illusion of religious belief is no longer conducive to individual or social welfare."[47]

In *Lying Truths*, Sir Hermann Bondi states that we have for too long lived with the myths that religious paranormal beliefs are altogether healthy.[48] In fact, he argues, at its roots, religious belief is a "serious and habit-forming evil." In making his case, Bondi even cites evidence that there are *fewer* criminals in atheist populations than in those harboring conventional religious paranormal beliefs. He concludes by saying: "Unhappily the widespread acceptance of the 'lying truth' that religion is a good thing is still delaying the complete success of the unifying and healing principle of tolerance."

One should not forget that religious and all reality-transcending beliefs are of overall survival value to our species. It just happens that intolerance, insensitivity to self and others, and destructiveness are accompaniments of paranormal believing. It would be quite easy to bolster that statement further by taking a historical look at wars and the astounding array of other techniques we have for destroying each other. Endless numbers of people have come to premature deaths as a result of someone or some group wanting to defend or propagate irrational beliefs. The sociologist Hugh Dalziel Duncan was quite right when he said that "all wars are conducted as holy wars."[49] In a similar vein, Rank regarded all wars as ideological dramatizations of our natural drive to deny immortality and to transcend the awesome and savage nature of creation.

Henry George, in *Social Problems*, captured the paramount importance of belief and the extent to which we will go in the defense of even the most irrational of beliefs: "No theory is too false, no fable too absurd, no superstition too degrading for acceptance when it has become imbedded in common belief. Men will submit themselves to torture and death, mothers will immolate their children, at the bidding of beliefs they thus accept."[50] George rightly specified that it is *commonly*-held beliefs that we shall follow to the point of self-destruction and/or genocide. We are relatively safe from people who hold minority beliefs. Our species can absorb the damage they do to themselves and others in the maintenance or defense of their beliefs. As tragic and pitiful as was the Jonestown massacre and group suicide, our species was not threatened in any real way by it. In fact, the human race could, and does, withstand small-scale tolls on our numbers as a result of a vast number of organized minority-belief systems. Paranormal beliefs become a serious danger only when such beliefs become *conventional*, when they become embodied in collective cultural consciousness, when they become *agreed-upon* untruths. Until recently, even conventional paranormal belief systems did not represent the possibility of the extinction of our entire species. Now they do. We can no longer afford to defy reality with paranormal belief. Early in our evolutionary past, paranormal believing was born from the collision of consciousness and reality. Despite some affordable costs, we solved that problem and flourished as a species. However, a new collision is taking place and the forces involved are moving so quickly that the final crash of our species may be unavoidable. What now faces us is the collision between paranormal belief and technology. The nuclear age has brought with it the means for us to obliterate our entire species in a defense of reality-transcending beliefs. It is true that all wars are "holy" wars; they all come down to cherished illusions and self-deceptions about earthly limitations. In that respect, all wars are "religious" wars.

The relationship between paranormal believing and our gravitation toward destructiveness is a curious one. We need to explore the dynamics of evil more deeply to see how a defiance of reality can turn us into creatures so eager to destroy each other and ourselves. Eugène Ionesco believed that it is the impossibility of achieving immortality that makes us continue to hate each other. This, he maintained, is despite our need for mutual love. In *The Denial of Death* Becker stated that "beyond ourselves we see chaos."[51] Our mortality is an aspect of the chaos that we run the risk of perceiving too clearly. In a similar vein to Ionesco, Becker proclaimed the human motto to be: "I am threatened with death – let us kill plentifully."[52] This is reminiscent of Caligula's comment in Camus' play *Caligula*: "How strange! When I don't kill, I feel alone." Caligula is frustrated and bent on killing since he is unable to transcend the Normal. To Caesonia he says: "All I need is for the impossible to be. The impossible! I've searched for it at the confines of the world, in the secret places of my heart . . . but it's always you I find, you only, confronting me."

Becker's sharp eye saw that *life makes people uncomfortable*, hence the serene accord with which they have defeated themselves throughout history. In the process of submitting to the other-than-normal we become "midwives of horror," very thirsty for each other's blood. Becker reasons that it is primarily our illusions about reality that we have to fear. However, we fear reality to such an extent that most of us refuse to ever see our dangerous illusions for what they are.

Ernest Becker died while working on *Escape from Evil*. Fortunately for us, his wife and friends did an excellent job of compiling and editing that partially completed manuscript so it could be made available to the public. In this final work, Becker detailed the paradoxical connection between our escape from reality and our sadly inevitable way of destroying what is around us. In so doing, he managed to bridge psychology and theology, and to pave the way for a totally new understanding of many social and psychological maladies. More importantly, he exposed the heaviest toll associated with the paranormal belief imperative. Paranormal believing makes us potential killers: good killers, well-intentioned killers, sometimes even holy killers – but killers none the less.

In addressing the nature of social evil, Becker credits Rank with having recognized that our paradoxical nature is the driving force underlying much of human destructiveness. We are "in the flesh and doomed with it." At the same time, we are "out of the flesh in the world of symbols and trying to continue on a heavenly flight."[53] We cannot do both. Becker sums up the dilemma that transforms us into dangerous worm-gods:

> The thing that makes man the most devastating animal that ever stuck his neck up into the sky is that he wants a stature and destiny that is impossible for an animal; he wants an earth that is not an earth but a heaven, and the price for this fantastic ambition is to make the earth an even more eager graveyard than it naturally is."[54]

Even though many of our reality-transcending paranormal beliefs would have us on a "heavenly flight," there is a sinister underside to our mental submission to the unreal: "The Devil himself seems to have contrived an instant puppet show with real live creatures . . . but there is no way to avoid the fatality of it . . . it is an animal's reaction to the majesty of creation."[55]

Becker writes that "men will take one another's heads because *their own heads* stick out and they feel exposed."[56] Specifically, they feel exposed to life and death. Wilhelm Reich astutely observed that all human belief has essentially the same message, namely that we are something other than animals.[57] That helps us to understand what Becker said in *The Denial of Death*: "No mistake – the turd is mankind's greatest threat."[58] We want a destiny somehow beyond, or different from the cold facts of creation. Our beliefs attempt to distort the apparent truth, which is that nothing makes sense, nothing rhymes, and that we are all rushing toward the soon to be forgotten compost heap.

In that respect, all ideology is of some value. A devil could be as useful as a god. An astrology message, a tree spirit, ESP, UFOlogy, or even the earth-bound ideologies we see today – they all battle against logic and reason. They all serve to convince us that our fate (even if only our earthly fate) is more than a wait in some *cage aux folles* where nothing really happens, where no one *really* goes anywhere, and where the self is no more than an absurd neurochemical wisp of absolutely no significance.

The only solution is to transcend the self and to create distance from the rational self. We take refuge in what is outside ourselves and outside of nature and the normal. However, it is exactly this *self-transcendence* that opens the door for destructiveness. It is the foundation for intolerance, insensitivity, and the other personality characteristics that make us the only creature regularly to destroy its own kind. It is also, as Reich saw, what enables leaders to get a ring through the noses of the masses and to lead them off to the ideological slaughter we have come to call war. Those who believed in Hitler and his prescription for a better world were simply engaging in a faulty earth-bound religion. Hitler was an excellent hypnotist who channeled the crowd's suggestibility into collective delusions that would scar the entire world. His belief system demanded as much irrationality as even the wildest of reality-distorting paranormal beliefs.

We typically regard self-transcendence as a desirable end that reflects an "elevated" level of consciousness. This probably stems from the use of the term in jargon related to contemporary quasi-religious practices such as transcendental meditation, yoga, and other "contentless" states to which many strive today. The term self-transcendence is used here in a broad sense. It refers to the way in which we must become removed from ourselves in order to live with distortions of reality. All counter-intelligence is dependent upon self-transcendence. Our most fundamental task is to escape at least that part of ourselves that could accurately perceive the chaotic and orderless world in which we live. In the *self-transcendent* everyday trance we are able to successfully transcend our two greatest enemies – the truth and ourselves. Up to a point, the more one can achieve self-transcendence the more "adjusted" one should be. We looked at research to support this. However, we also saw that self-transcendent (or paranormal) belief was associated with the personal characteristics that lead to destructiveness and cruelty.

We are beginning to sound like heartless machines. This could be because we truly are machines, or at least parts of the machinery of culture. Paul Valéry made the piercing observation that "man is only man at the surface – remove his skin, dissect, and immediately you come to machinery." Arthur Koestler's *The Ghost in the Machine* helps us to understand why self-transcendent belief makes us into such savage animals or machines. He describes us as "cheerful ostriches" since our beliefs cause us to "successfully offend our reasoning faculties."[59] More specifically, Koestler compares human beings to robots and machines because of the "dimming of awareness and the loss of the subjective experience of freedom" that accompanies self-transcendent beliefs. Our evolutionary "schizophysiology" demands that we entertain both the rational and the irrational, the real and the unreal. To do this, Koestler speaks of the need for the "un-selfing of the self."[60]

According to Koestler, self-transcendence and self-transcending beliefs require us to maintain a "mild form of hypnotic anesthesia."[61] If we can achieve what he calls "mild somnambulism" or "spellboundness," we can then effectively transcend ourselves and adopt the suggestions of culture. We are then *unfree* enough to believe what would be foreign to someone totally *in touch* with one's self. The herd and the group mentality is formed in this way. Once self-transcended, people behave and believe in a *single-minded* manner. Self-transcendence, to Koestler, enables a group to suspend individual differences in perception and to anesthetize each member's critical faculties. In turn, we are successfully transformed into a common denominator that can share single-mindedness and simple-mindedness.[62]

Self-transcending paranormal belief is the most desired form of what Koestler calls simple-mindedness. An infinitely complex situation of complete chaos and unanswerable questions is made simple. Answers, explanations, guidelines and directions are all to be found in counter-intelligent or simple-minded beliefs. Without such beliefs, Koestler holds that the human race would be made up of "mean little islands." Without the ideological glue to bind us to others, our destructiveness would be acted out on a *private* and individual basis. Koestler feels that we would be "mean" and "selfish" if we did not manage to become anesthetized by transcendent belief. However, he states that we would become much more mean and more destructive as "cheerful" ostriches who are spellbound by reality-distorting beliefs. Our ability to retreat from ourselves in the service of cognitively biased beliefs is what forms the cornerstone of man's inhumanity to man.

Becker, more than Koestler, emphasizes that mentally unanesthetized people would be literally scared out of their wits. We must transcend ourselves in order to effectively employ self-deception in converting panic into the illusion of order. Yet, he also contends that "it is the *disguise* of panic that makes men live in ugliness."[63] This concept is reinforced in the following words from *Escape from Evil*: "Man's urge to self-transcendence, his devotion to a cause, has made more butchery than private aggressiveness in history . . . "[64] Becker goes on to say that we "hunger for believable words that dress life in convincing meaning." However, he reiterates Koestler's ideas in the following statement which highlights the danger inherent in these words we are dying to believe:

It is not aggressive drives that have taken the greatest toll in history, but rather 'unselfish devotion,' 'hyper-dependence combined with suggestibility'. . . . Man is less driven by adrenalin than he is drugged by symbols, by cultural belief systems . . . . Wars are fought for words.[65]

The words for which we are prepared to lay down our lives and that of others are those that form our self-transcending and reality-transcending lies. However, in transcending ourselves we open our minds to "closed" group ideology. Becker addressed the paradox of self-transcendence. We abandon ourselves to group self-transcending beliefs in order to defeat the ultimate evil, namely reality. Part of that "evil" is our mortality. In that regard, Becker acknowledges that we are "willing to die in order not to die." We also "kill lavishly out of the sublime joy of heroic triumph over [that] evil."[66] Becker would agree with Pascal's sentiment that all people, by their very nature, hate each other. That is because we naturally despise life. Ironically, we manage to love by creating death. For Becker, sadism naturally counteracts our fear of life and our fear of death. He writes that we are "an animal who needs the spectacle of death in order to open ourselves to love."[67] However, in conquering the evil of life and reality, we end up creating evil and death. This same twisted fate is recorded by Hugh Dalziel Duncan:

> As we wound and kill our enemy in the field and slaughter his women and children in their homes, our love for each other deepens. We become comrades in arms; our hatred of each other is being purged in sufferings of our enemy.[68]

Fromm saw human aggression as the result of a mechanical "necrophilia" (love of death) that has emerged in contemporary Western society. Becker criticized Fromm, and rightly so, for his undue optimism. Although Fromm recognized that we are attracted to death and consequently verging on a nuclear suicide of the human species, he also maintained that hope is to be found in the "biophiles."[69] These biophiles are the "lovers of life" who could represent the seeds of a new society with a new consciousness based on tolerance, non-violence, and cooperation. Becker wavered on the issue of hope. In his earlier writings, he resisted the temptation to say that there is hope for the human animal. Instead he denounced Fromm's biophiles as people who were successfully *deluded* about the true nature of life. That is, we find hope only when we can achieve normal insanity in the form of self-transcending distortions of reality. This pathological mental health is obtained when we can sufficiently transcend ourselves to believe in the occurrence of the impossible. Therefore, it is in the nature of *everyone* to seek self-transcendence in the form of the various beliefs offered by culture. In the same way, self-transcendence makes *everyone* into potential necrophiles. Furthermore, the better one is at self-transcending self-deception, the more deadly one becomes. Another paradox is that we are always *righteous* killers.

The specific mechanisms by which self-transcendence gives way to destructiveness are not hard to determine. First of all, out-of-touchness with self makes empathy with others nearly impossible. To empathize with others, one must feel and know oneself. Compassion and tolerance for others is born from *self*-awareness. Elie Wiesel was referring to our fundamentally inhumane natures when he made his famous statement that *man is not human*. In order to be human to ourselves and others, we must truly know and feel that we are earthlings, and that we have an *earthly* fate. Self-transcending beliefs make us something other than mere animals, and often something *less* than animals.

From intimate *self*-knowledge and *self*-contact there springs a deep sadness for oneself and for one's inevitably sad fate. In striving to deny and transcend the macabre truth that hounds us we become less aware of ourselves and others. People who see themselves as something (or part of something) more than doomed animals also fail to see others as sharing a similar fate. We transcend our animal nature and destinies when we engage in transcendent beliefs. But in so doing, we become animals in the worst sense of the word. The well-known saying "men are dogs to men" reflects the effects of self-deception and a detachment from ourselves. In self-forgetting we forget others. Becker writes: "There is nothing wrong with illusion that is creative. Up to a point, of course; the point at which the illusion lies about something very important, such as human nature."[70] In seeing ourselves as a small part of the compost pile of creation, we have a common bond with our fellow human beings and all of nature. It is the bond of tears, regret, mourning, and terror. Still, in that cheerless connection to each other we find a responsibility to self and others that is incompatible with destructiveness. However, as self-transcended worm-gods we are bound to our illusions. We are then not really human, nor are those around us. Ironically, by denying our nothingness we become nothing – or at least nothing of value. Self-transcendence in all its forms causes alienation from self and from others. We can only destroy others if we are alienated from them. The same holds true for the way we behave toward ourselves. The most the self-transcended individual can achieve is mindless membership in the culture club of belief. But then the blood really flows as potentially "mean little islands" become soldiers in a larger killing machine. That is when the door is opened to destruction on a wholesale level, usually in the service of some ideology. Like all ideology, it is life-giving and life-taking in nature.

When Koestler speaks of the "un-selfing" of the self, he is referring to the phenomenon of *deindividuation* which occurs when a person transcends himself/herself with unworldly beliefs. Deindividuation can be defined as the process whereby external inputs lessen self-awareness and concern for self and others, causing a release of disinhibited behavior.[71] Of course, the "external inputs" that are of significance here are the cultural suggestions that form the building-blocks of our self-transcending paranormal beliefs. A large body of research shows that people become more aggressive and destructive when they become deindividuated. The reason is that reduced levels of self-awareness make people less aware and less concerned about the pain they inflict on others. We saw before that dampened self-awareness was an aspect of the self-transcendence involved in paranormal believing. It follows, as the research indicates, that self-transcended people are less inhibited about causing suffering in others.

Steven Prentice-Dunn and Ronald Rogers at the University of Alabama have spearheaded some of the research on this important topic. They subdivide self-awareness into private self-awareness and public self-awareness.[72] Private self-awareness refers to the tendency to focus on personal, private, or covert aspects of oneself, such as one's own thoughts, emotions, and perceptions. In contrast, public self-awareness involves the awareness of oneself as a social object, and a concern about how one fits into the social environment. People vary considerably in terms of the amounts of private or public self-awareness that they possess. Prentice-Dunn and Rogers experimentally decreased the degree of private self-awareness in order to promote a state of deindividuation in their subjects. To achieve this, subjects were made to direct attention away from themselves and onto cooperative tasks designed to foster group cohesiveness. In addition, the participants were specifically instructed to focus attention outward and not on themselves. These researchers obtained valuable evidence that lowered self-awareness results in a state of deindividuation. In turn, they found that deindividuated people are more likely to engage in collective aggression. In their study, aggression was measured by the intensity of electric shock that the subjects were willing to give to an anonymous individual.

Granted, laboratory studies like this are highly contrived. None the less, they add some "hard" support for the theoretical speculations about the dangers of all behaviors that lead one away from oneself. Paranormal believing is one such behavior. Self-transcendence, or "un-selfing," is the universal method by which members of our species lower an awareness of themselves. However, as we close our minds on ourselves, we seem to close our minds and hearts on others.

Another team of investigators, led by Michael Scheier at Carnegie-Mellon University, help us to understand the link between self-transcendence and destructiveness.[73] Their research was devoted to the relationship between self-awareness and suggestibility. They discovered that human suggestibility depends on a certain degree of *unawareness* of self. The degree of this unawareness determines the extent to which a person can utilize an external, in contrast to an internal, frame of reference in establishing one's perceptions, judgments, and interpretations of one's environment. As we become less self-aware, we are increasingly inclined to adopt external suggestions, however inaccurate or in contradiction to our private selves they might be. As Prentice-Dunn and Rogers demonstrated, the self-unaware person will abandon personal standards of morality and follow the suggested guidelines for action coming from an external source. The reason that self-unaware people will engage in unwarranted aggression is because they have surrendered the personal codes that would determine their behavior in the self-aware state.

Scheier's research team carried out a clever experiment to test the hypothesis that self-unawareness underlies suggestibility and the acceptance of misleading information. The object of the study was to determine the degree to which they could influence the person's perception and experience. They used a group of men as subjects. Each one was instructed that they were going to view some slides. The researchers experimentally manipulated the anticipations of one group by suggesting to them that they would not find the slides arousing or stimulating. Having done that, they showed each man slides of beautiful, naked women. As expected, they found that their suggestions caused the men to override their own perceptions and to report less arousal than men who were not given the suggestion regarding non-arousal.

Scheier also wanted to know if it was possible to reduce this suggestibility effect by increasing a person's self-focus. To do this, they took a different sample of men and showed them the slides on a specially constructed projection screen. This consisted of 50 percent reflection glass which meant that these men could see themselves before and after the slide show, as well as between each slide. It was hypothesized that this reflection of oneself would reduce suggestibility by increasing self-awareness. As predicted, the men in this high self-awareness condition were not as "fooled" into accepting misinformation as were the other subjects. Confirmation was obtained for the theory that suggestibility is reliant on an "un-selfed" or unaware self.

If suggestibility is the evolutionary feat that enables self-transcending paranormal belief, we should expect to find that believers are less self-aware than non-believers. Earlier, we saw that this is the case. The greater destructiveness that we observe in paranormal believers is undoubtedly a function of the unawareness of self that accompanies suggestibility. Non-believers are less suggestible and more self-aware. However, they are, as we have seen, more neurotic.

What a choice we humans have! To be blind and destructive or to be neurotic. That is the question.

There is truth in the world. Much of it is bitter and unsettling. Self-transcending beliefs allow us to close our eyes and retreat into collective illusions. When we become "unselfed" and deindividuated, however, we apparently lose interest in protecting one another. The amount of responsibility we take for our fellow creatures diminishes in proportion to our estrangement from ourselves. Throughout our history, the scales balanced in favor of the blindness that we find in self-transcending paranormal beliefs. Unfortunately, killing technology has now placed a new price tag on our drive to be strangers to ourselves and strangers to reality. Our entire species may self-deceive its way into extinction. The paranormal belief imperative cannot absorb the methods of destruction that we have now made available to ourselves. Ironically, what Becker called our "victory over human limitation" has become our greatest limitation and our most important challenge.

Be it too late or not, there is a lot that can be accomplished by viewing ourselves in the context of our inherent urge for paranormal belief and self-transcendence. We stand on the threshold of giant theoretical strides concerning the essential nature of ourselves. Fromm may be right that we have become killers of time, as well as killers of each other. But, if we realize that our stay on this planet is nearing an end, we may be inclined to place a new value on the time remaining. One thing we can do is to apply our new insights to a better understanding of certain kinds of psychological suffering.

# 6 *The Clumsy Lie*

Ernest Becker recognized that mental illness is a consequence of failing to *misinterpret* the world in which we find ourselves. In *The Denial of Death* he makes the astute observation that, "Madmen are the greatest reasoners we know . . . there is no one more logical than the lunatic."[1]

This chapter will attempt to re-shape our understanding of some forms of mental illness that affect large numbers of our species. The types of disorders that are relevant here will collectively be called "monoideistic" disorders. An exceptionally good example of this type of psychological disturbance is anorexia nervosa. Other monoideistic disorders that I shall mention are obsessions, compulsions, and paranoia. All have a common basis. They are all problems of misdirected suggestibility, of misdirected "religion." Sadly, the success rate of current therapies is very low with these forms of psychopathology. Any advance in the understanding and treatment of such problems would represent an important contribution to the field of mental health.

Not all of us are able to attain what Kierkegaard called "fictitious mental health." Even if a culture is intact and doing its job well, some of us seem to have trouble using conventional, culture-based ideology to limit ourselves to that safe dose of reality. We now need to ask at what level of illusion the human being functions best. Also, what are the mental health consequences of failing to find effective systems of self-deception? Modern psychology has largely failed to deal with these critical questions. Becker's answer to these can form the core of a new framework by which we can begin to understand mental illness:

> In order to function normally, a man has to achieve from the beginning a serious *constriction* of the world and of himself. We can say that the essence of normality is the *refusal of reality*! What we call neurosis enters precisely at this point: Some people have more trouble with their lies than others. The world is too much for them, and the techniques that they have developed for holding it at bay and cutting it down to size finally begin to choke the person. This is neurosis in a nutshell: *the miscarriage of clumsy lies about reality.*[2]

Certain mental disturbances have no history of trauma, mistreatment, or conflict. Such is the case with the disorders I shall mention. What is even more opposed to the usual conflict model that psychologists use is the fact that those who suffer from these disorders frequently have very desirable social and family histories. Beyond that, they are often highly intelligent and demonstrate superior ability in many areas of life functioning. I want to argue that certain categories of mental illness are best understood in the context of our "theological" natures.

We have already looked at research that showed that "poor" paranormal believers do not seem to compensate for their deficit with other paranormal beliefs. We did see, however, that they suffer more symptoms of mental illness. Many of these symptoms represent an attempt to *constrict* or limit one's perceptions of reality. I believe Becker was correct in his assertion that many types of mental disturbances are "private religions," *substitute* religions that narrow and reduce reality down to manageable size. In its reduced stature, reality can be understood and *controlled.* They are "clumsy" because clinical symptoms are less effective than the "*normal* cultural pathology" (Freud's term) that most of us use to distort the world.

In his research into the causes of religious conversion, Heirich concludes that such conversion should be understood as "an assertion of a sense of ultimate grounding, one that provides a clear basis for understanding reality . . . and orients and orders experience."[3] That is a good description of the function served by many "private religions" that are expressed as symptoms of mental disturbance. Freud saw that by obtaining the pathology of the entire culture, one could avoid personal (or clinical) pathologies. For some reason, people who do not self-transcend via orthodox cultural belief systems often rely on the weakly rooted and

ineffective *private* escapes that we regard as mental illness.
Anorexia nervosa is one such escape.

## Thinness: an unlikely god

I am convinced that anorexia nervosa holds the key to a
breakthrough in our understanding of both normal and abnormal
behavior. The disorder makes almost no sense in the context of
the usual theories we use to explain human behavior. Prior to the
onset of their symptoms, anorexics are typically described as
"ideal" children. Until this disorder transforms them into a mere
physical and psychological shell of their former selves, they
usually outperform their peers. They engender the pride and
admiration of most people they meet.

Anorexics almost always come from intact, upper-middle-class
families with highly concerned and caring parents who involve
themselves very closely with their children. Cases of child abuse,
neglect, or deprivation of any sort are virtually non-existent. In
fact, the girls who later become anorexic tend to be *very* close
to their parents, and in particular their mothers. These mothers
are intimately involved with almost all aspects of their daughters'
lives. In fact, the relationships are so close that the mother and
daughter become psychologically "enmeshed." Consequently,
the daughter does not have much chance to develop a sense of
self. She does not experience herself as an independent, "indi-
viduated," or autonomous person separate from her mother.
Essentially, the anorexic has it so "good" that she does not
develop the personal resources that would enable her to cope
with adult responsibilities. That is why the disorder is usually
precipitated in mid-adolescence, the time of transition from child
to adult. The realities of the adult world are perceived (often on an
unconscious level) as overwhelming and potentially debilitating.

With their limited coping resources, the world seems incomprehensible and overcomplicated. They "know" on some level
that they have no answers to the many adult questions that are
now being asked. They sense that they are ill-equipped to make
the choices and decisions that will take them into adulthood. To
the would-be anorexic, the approaching "real world" appears as a
terrifying chaos. The encroaching reality is *unmanageably* large.
The way in which the budding anorexic adapts to this threat is to
*shrink* her world, by *narrowing* dramatically the focus of her
perceptions. The entire foundation of her existence becomes the

pursuit of thinness – *perfect* thinness, *infinite* thinness. She creates a new miniature reality with simple black-and-white answers. Everything that happens from that point on is filtered through her one commandment: thou shalt be thin. In that tiny perceptual set, she finds psychological sanctuary. She has defeated reality and conquered the endless possibilities that were about to consume her.

This formulation of the psychodynamics of anorexia nervosa can be traced back to the brilliant early writings of Hilda Bruch.[4] The cornerstone of this view is that the anorexic's symptoms are an attempt to attain a sense of control and order in her life. By reducing the *scope* of her perceptions, she is able to *ignore* the rest of the world. Arthur Koestler shows a similar understanding of anorexia nervosa when he describes it as a form of "maladaptive specialization."[5] By "specialization," Koestler is referring to the same sort of *constriction* of reality about which Becker speaks. All of us must "specialize," constrict, and transform our perceptions of the world. In so doing, we invent and exaggerate the importance of fictions about our new reality. That is the primary task of us creatures of the paranormal. It is the essence of religion. The anorexic has taken on a *maladaptive* religion. It is, of course, maladaptive because perfect thinness is a life-threatening god – a truly murderous god of health!

A "religious" theory can explain the purpose of anorexic symptoms. It can also explain why these healthy young people turn specifically to thinness in order to alter their understanding and perception of the world. It can also help to answer other vital questions about the development of the disorder. For example, why is it that *those* particular young women fall victim to that disorder? Also, why in their cases were conventional, culturally-rooted paranormal lies unable to do the job of distorting reality for them? Why did they need to make drastic further modifications to their perceptions of the world? In other words, what was it about these people that prevented them from being pacified and sustained with *normal* cultural pathology? Why is anorexia nervosa prevalent and increasing in some parts of the world and totally non-existent in others? A "religious" formulation can answer these puzzling questions concerning such a disorder. But the answer to all these questions must take us back to a discussion of human suggestibility and the manner in which culture interacts with our innate suggestibility.

I can recall the exact moment when I realized that anorexia nervosa was actually a form of defective paranormal self-deception affecting the innate suggestibility process. I was talking to an anorexic student of mine whom I had come to care about very much. It was a private college and, not atypically, had more than its share of anorexics. This young woman had seen the best specialists in the country and had been hospitalized many times as a result of her quest for thinness. I was aware of how low the success rate was in the treatment of anorexia nervosa. Even those who show improvement frequently lapse back into their symptoms. And the supposedly "cured" ones experience residual effects well into their adult lives. This particular person was certainly no exception. Her financially well-off family had spent a king's ransom on her treatments and she was only continuing to deteriorate.

In my office, she was telling me that she had eaten four grains of rice for lunch. She described how she isolated each grain of rice on her plate and cut each grain into four or five pieces before eating them. As she spoke, I found myself wanting to scream at her, to shake her violently, to slap her, and wake her up to what she was doing to herself. I then thought of all the therapists and health professionals who must have pulled their hair out in trying to help this fine person. It occurred to me how totally *inaccessible* she was. She absorbed *nothing* of what anyone was *suggesting* or prescribing to her. Then, like the proverbial light bulb flicking on, it dawned on me that she was in a trance. She was hypnotized! At the same time, I saw that she was, and for some time had been, totally *non-suggestible*! Her therapies had all failed for that reason. One has to bring a certain degree of suggestibility into a treatment setting in order to be influenced by the therapist. She had no free or available suggestibility!

I had the pieces of the puzzle, but did not know then how they would fit together. One immediate theoretical knot was that the suggestibility model appeared logically backwards. If anorexia nervosa was, in fact, an altered state of consciousness similar to hypnosis, the anorexic would be highly suggestible. What I was seeing was the opposite – an absence of suggestibility.

I decided to measure suggestibility levels in a group of anorexic individuals. The pilot study I did then showed that they were, as my intuition told me, considerably less suggestible than a similar group of non-anorexics. The logical impasse loomed larger than ever. If anorexia nervosa were a trance phenomenon, how would they become initially entranced if they were so non-suggestible? A thorough search of the psychological literature revealed precious little on any possible connection between suggestibility and anorexia nervosa, or any other disorder for that matter. I did run across some descriptions of anorexics as "robot-like" and "programmed" in their behavior, not unlike hypnotic subjects who had virtually no will and no sense of self.[6] While not helping much to put the whole picture together, these references reassured me that I might be on the right theoretical track.

It was not until I ran across the writings of Mordecai Kaffman that my ideas began to fall into place. Kaffman, an Israeli psychiatrist, proposed that an entire class of mental disturbance was *auto-hypnotic* in nature.[7] He refers to these disorders as "monoideisms," and includes anorexia nervosa among them. Monoideisms, to Kaffman, are highly localized patterns of thought. They have "repetitive and *constrictive* thematic content controlling a great portion of the subjects' self-language, which affects cognitions, affective reactions, and interpersonal relationships." He also uses the term "monomotivation" to describe the behavior of people suffering from monoideistic disorders. A monomotivation is a fixed, singular "dominant idea" with an associated compulsive behavior pattern that becomes the complete preoccupation of the victim.

Kaffman hypothesizes that people with monoideistic disorders are in an altered state of consciousness characterized by this "closed system of thought." Their semi-automatic thinking and their "inflexible belief constructs" are a result of the "commands" these people give to themselves. According to this theory, the auto-hypnotic monoideism serves to relieve anxiety through a process of emotional dissociation or deindividuation. The affected individual is "shutting off the mind from external reality."[8] As the process develops, the closed system of autosuggestion causes a type of "cognitive feedback" that further enhances suggestibility. Once in the grips of the auto-hypnotic monoideism, the person surrenders totally to the dictates of the recurring cognitions. The presence of the "single ruling motivation" destroys all ability to concentrate on anything else. They lack the volition or will to resist the self-induced hypnotic state that involves "*blind* belief and *uncritical* obedience" to the one ruling motivation and ideation.

In outlining the major features of his ideas, Kaffman captures better than anyone the process of symptom development in anorexia nervosa. He builds the theoretical groundwork to support the view that anorexia nervosa and related disorders are forms of trance. Specifically, they are *self-maintained* states of *auto-*

suggestion. For the first time that I was aware, a specific mental disorder was made traceable to dysfunctions in the normal mental processes that have evolved to generate *adaptive* constrictions of reality. Whereas certain socially sanctioned paranormal belief systems are "healthy" specializations (or distortions) of one's cognitive world, anorexia nervosa and similar syndromes are *maladaptive channelings of suggestibility.* They are clumsy "private" religions that employ verifiably false illusions about the world. Unlike traditional religion in which people bask in life-giving *conventional* insanity, the private god of the anorexic causes this person to become stranded on a lonely island of misdirected conviction and devotion. The anorexic is alone. That, in itself, makes it impossible for thinness to be a successful god or a successful hiding place. Good gods, as we saw, need a *collective* nod.

Still, for this model to make sense, it seems one should observe *higher* levels of suggestibility in someone with a disorder like anorexia nervosa. All evidence was pointing to *lower* levels. The solution occurred to me while reading about the striking personality contrasts that can be observed in anorexics before and after the actual onset of the disorder. Before the disorder emerges, the young person (95 percent are female) is typically described as cooperative, socially responsive and engaging, meticulous and perfectionistic, polite, easily accessible, impressionable, desiring to please, and so forth. Once the symptoms become manifest, however, a Jekyll and Hyde transformation takes place. Many parents say that they become entirely "different people."

Health professionals describe the individual in the fully developed anorexic condition as stubborn, uncooperative, "closed off," unresponsive, secretive, resistant to change, deceptive, and "in a world of their own." Large mood swings frequently take the place of the former even-natured behavior pattern. In the anorexic state, the victim often alternates between severe dejection and self-deprecation on the one hand, and righteous indignation combined with euphoria on the other.

It became clear that the pre-onset (i.e., before the disorder is precipitated) individual has many characteristics of a person who would be labeled "suggestible." It was also more than obvious that post-onset people (i.e., the anorexic herself) are the epitome of *non-suggestibility.* In the brief transition from "normal" to anorexic, much of the person's suggestibility disappears. The reduction in apparent suggestibility levels seems too extreme to dismiss as just a by-product of the disorder. That is when I realized that one *purpose* of anorexia nervosa is to *absorb* excessive amounts of "loose" suggestibility. That is, the anorectic symptoms function to *bind* suggestibility for which no "healthy" channel has been found. Anorexia nervosa is a conversion to a maladaptive "religion" and an inferior type of god. The process and cognitive mechanisms involved are the same as anyone funneling their suggestibility into any contorted perceptions of reality. The important difference is that the anorexic has left the *cultural* track. Somehow, culture has failed to direct that person's suggestiblity into conventional belief systems which could provide the "normal" illusion of control and order. The "cognitive biases" of the anorexia nervosa victim are not *self-serving*. They are self-destructive.

Two possible explanations presented themselves to me. One was that the pre-onset anorexic is *hyper-suggestible* and, as such, normal cultural suggestibility channels (e.g., religion) are not capable of absorbing that quantity of suggestibility. In that case, the anorexic-to-be would be forced to invent *more* religion in the form of a "private" religion such as anorexia nervosa. That does not necessarily mean this individual abandons other cultural fictions. Rather, she is forced to *supplement* what culture can afford her in the way of self-transcendence and reality-transcendence. In this respect, such people make their own magic. They find *their own* shelter from the chaos impinging on them. Thinness, as their monoideism and monomotivation, becomes the mental linchpin on which hinge all interpretations of reality. Good and evil, right and wrong, friend and foe – all these derive from the "trance logic" of an autosuggestive disorder, such as anorexia nervosa.[9] The second possibility was that Western culture has become ineffective as a psychic defense mechanism and that it lacks the institutions and inner structure to cope with even modestly elevated levels of suggestibility. I realized that both of these possibilities could be tested.

If anorexia nervosa were a private constriction of reality in order to bind excessive suggestibility, people *on the verge* of the disorder would be seen to have elevated levels of suggestibility. To explore this, it was necessary to isolate a group of "subclinical" anorexics. That is a term that some researchers are using to describe people who have many of the signs of anorexia nervosa, but who have not yet developed the full-blown syndrome. A colleague and I administered the Eating Attitude Test[10] to a

large group of teenage women. This test provides an indication of
one's risk of developing anorexia nervosa by assessing the degree
of concern for body weight and inclination to adopt radical
weight control methods.

We isolated a sample who scored above the critical cut-off score
that indicates the presence of anorectic behavior, and then
eliminated those subjects who were actually anorexic. That left us
with a sample of young women who appeared to be *predisposed*
toward developing anorexia nervosa. We then measured their
suggestibility levels with the Harvard Suggestibility Scale and
compared their scores with a non-anorexic control group. The
pre-anorexic subjects had significantly *higher* suggestibility levels.[11]
That provided direct support for the theory that anorexia nervosa
may be a psychological adaptation to free-floating hyper-suggestibility. The fact that fully developed anorexics had lower levels of
suggestibility then made sense. The syndrome itself effectively
utilized all available suggestibility in maintaining irrational
beliefs and behavioral devotion to the one thing that can now
give order to chaos, uncertainty, and personal ineffectiveness.

People with anorexia nervosa are religious converts in every
sense of the word. Their devotion to their weight-related belief
systems are more extreme than even "born again" religious
fanatics. They have enormous amounts of suggestibility tied up
in a highly focused and singular paranormal belief system. These
beliefs are *para*normal because their beliefs regarding the powers
of thinness to remedy the world are completely ill-founded. They
would never derive from information extracted from the *real*
world. They far exceed rationality and logic in making thinness
and food refusal the yardstick by which to evaluate and interpret
all life-events.

People with poorly developed *assumptive* worlds become ripe
for religious conversion. The would-be anorexic is lacking exactly
that – a set of assumptions and "answers" that enable him/her to
impose order on chaos and uncertainty. Thinness, as a god and
singular cognitive frame of reference, is a fallible one-dimensional
assumption that is untrue. What is worse for the anorexic is that
this god does not even *work* in the sense that the person can carry
on productively. Beyond that, the extreme unconventional nature
of this oversimplistic religion forces the anorexic into a characteristic
social withdrawal. Nevertheless, the anorexic would, and often
does, die as the result of a devotion to the god of thinness. These
people are almost impossible to treat effectively, because they do

not *want* to be cured. They are no longer open in the least to the suggestions of therapists, family members, or peers. All their irrational and religious eggs are in one basket, so to speak. Anyone trying to take that away from them represents an ultimate threat. Religion, albeit aberrant religion, is the hardest thing to take from anyone. And, as we shall see, the half-hearted therapies used by Western psychologists pose little threat to the defensive cognitive armor of the anorexic.

Another feature of the anorexic syndrome suggests that we are dealing with a well-entrenched "religious" disorder. At a recent meeting of the American Society for Pharmacology, Mary Ann Marrazzi and Daniel L'Abbe revealed findings which suggest that anorexics are "high" on endorphins. Their laboratory studies detected elevated opioid (endorphin) activity in the cerebrospinal fluid of people with anorexia nervosa. I believe this is another important clue to show that anorexia nervosa operates exactly like religion. This may also help to explain why the anorexic is not amenable to therapeutic intervention, since these opiates constitute such powerful self-reinforcers. We saw previously that engagement in suggestibility absorbing behavior results in endorphin rewards by the brain. That may be one cause for the heightened levels of endorphins in anorexics. That would constitute the exact method by which religious and other paranormal belief systems are probably rewarded on a brain level. Therefore, like the true believer, the anorexic may be strongly addicted to endorphins. It is little wonder the success rate is so unfortunately low with anorexics. A "cure" entails taking away their religion as well as their addiction, a formidable task for even the most skilled of clinicians.

By viewing anorexia nervosa as an auto-hypnotic trance phenomenon, we can also explain the drastic body image distortions that one observes in the anorexic. That can best be understood as a feature of hypnotic dissociation. Such perceptual peculiarities can easily become manifest in certain highly suggestible people.

More support for anorexia nervosa as a disturbance of suggestibility comes from a study of environmental factors that influence suggestibility levels. For instance, it would be reasonable to ask why it is only people from such specific "ideal" backgrounds who develop suggestibility levels that exceed the channeling capabilities of culture. One must also wonder why it is usually upper-middle-class, over-monitored young women who are more prone to develop elevated suggestibility levels. An innovative study by Thomas Long sheds important light on this question. He examined suggestibility and hypnotic susceptibility as a function of how positive or negative were the early life experiences of people.[12] He found that very positive, conventional, and conflict-free early life-experiences were *positively* correlated with suggestibility and hypnotic susceptibility. Long wrote that "intimate" parental involvement in the social and personal lives of children appeared to enhance suggestibility.

In *The Evolution of Human Consciousness*, J. H. Crook also touches on the inherent dangers associated with intrusive parental involvement: "The excessive introjection of parental values has several disadvantages . . . it reduces the likelihood of a flexible and assertive response to social change . . . "[13] Although he was speaking generally, it is as if Crook were referring specifically to the dynamics of anorexia. Anorexia nervosa victims have lost virtually *all* flexibility and *all* ability to assert themselves in response to incipient life changes. Paralyzed in the face of monumental and overwhelming realities, they must opt to limit the size of their worlds. Kierkegaard writes in *The Sickness unto Death* that the average person must "*tranquilize itself with the trivial.*"[14] Most of us suffer that "sickness" in socially acceptable and health-enhancing ways. Anorexia nervosa sufferers do what we all do when overwhelmed by reality, but their method of trimming reality cripples their abilities to function effectively.

There is still another very interesting feature to anorexia nervosa. It exists in only certain cultures. More remarkable is the fact that certain non-Western cultures have disorders that are also suggestibility-based, but whose symptoms are different. So, let us look at monoideistic disorders in a cross-cultural perspective.

In one respect, anorexia nervosa is a *culture-bound* syndrome. That term is used to describe any type of psychopathology that only exists in one culture or one type of culture. A number of cross-cultural psychologists have reported on the complete absence of anorexia nervosa in a number of non-Western societies.[15] Numerous other types of mental disorders are limited to Western society as well. Other cultures have culture-bound syndromes of their own. Thus, they have mental disorders that exist there and not in our own culture. The case of anorexia nervosa is especially interesting because it seems to have counterparts in societies that do not have anorexia nervosa. A comparison of anorexia nervosa and a disorder such as koro could serve to delineate the role that culture plays in the formation of monoideistic psychological symptoms. *Koro* is a mental disturbance with which most Westerners are not familiar. It is a rare "depersonalization" disorder that afflicts some men in parts of South East Asia, Indonesia, Malaysia, and southern China.[16] In the Chinese language it is known as *suo-yang*, which means "shrinking penis." It is aptly labeled, because the men who suffer from this disorder firmly believe that their penises are shrinking and disappearing into their abdomens. The unfortunate victims of koro experience great distress as a result of the ever-present belief that this vital anatomical equipment is dwindling away. As a result, they spend a good deal of their time studying its size and attempting to determine if it has continued to shrink. This is frequently accompanied by vigorous tugging and pulling, sometimes to the point of inflicting damage to the abused organ.

At first, the similarities between koro and anorexia nervosa may not be obvious. But, as one studies the scarce literature on the subject, the overlap becomes clear. In fact, I am convinced that koro is *etiologically* the same, but *symptomatically* different from, anorexia nervosa. That is a fanciful way of saying that the same factors *cause* both anorexia nervosa and koro, but that the symptoms take on a different form. As one studies koro, one encounters reports of body-image distortion virtually identical to that in anorexia nervosa. The only difference with koro is that the body image disturbance is localized to the penis and reversed – the reversal involving the koro sufferer perceiving a part of the body to be smaller than it actually is; the anorexic perceiving her body to be *larger* than it is.

Many other common features emerge as one studies the two in tandem. They are both culture-bound disorders that affect individuals with similar personality structures. Behavioral descriptions of people in the pre-onset koro condition are often remarkably like those previously mentioned concerning the pre-onset anorexic. Prior to the emergence of the disorder, koro sufferers display many of the same socially desirable traits that characterize the pre-anorexic person. The "psychosomatic" family backgrounds of those who develop koro tend to be ones that foster dependency and do not allow for independent thought, *self*-directed action, or the development of a sense of an *autonomous* self. In many instances, the family backgrounds of those with koro are such that one would expect them to develop elevated suggestibility levels. In fact, many of the accompanying symptoms in koro are of a "hysterical" nature, the sort of symptoms frequently observed in more suggestible individuals. Both disorders tend to be precipitated in the face of impending social and environmental demands with which the individual feels incapable of meeting. Each disorder involves a monoideism in the form of a recurrent preoccupying thought, and each has related rituals or monomotivations. In that respect, both disorders seem suggestibility-based and to be attempts to *constrict* the person's perceptual world. Both are "private religions" which limit the person to a much smaller version of reality.

Anorexia nervosa and koro also involve phobic-level apprehensions concerning cultural taboos. This, in fact, explains the vastly different symptoms that emerge to absorb the free suggestibility. When conventional cultural myths and belief systems fail to convert suggestibility into pacifying methods by which to make sense of the world, the individual falls back on whatever cultural suggestions are most prevalent. In Western society, one of the strongest and all-pervasive suggestions is "be thin." For adolescent girls, one could argue that it is the *most* powerful of all cultural suggestions to which they are exposed. That suggestion is accompanied by the message that "all will be well" if one is thin enough. Normally, such cultural suggestions would be of secondary importance to what should be the primary suggestibility-absorbing ones that form the cultural shield against a clear perception of reality. As such, a healthy society with intact religious paranormal beliefs should not witness epidemics of "monoideistic" disorders. That is precisely why anorexia nervosa, in its present form, was extremely rare prior to the erosion of traditional religious paranormal beliefs that began in the late seventeenth and eighteenth centuries. The numbers of monoideistic disorders have grown in proportion to the breakdown in traditional cultural myths. Be that as it may, the fact remains that "be thin" looms larger than any other cultural suggestion to the young people vulnerable to anorexia nervosa. When they burrow into their private religion of thinness, they are adopting what is culturally in front of them. It is perfectly understandable that the exceptionally suggestible Western person turns to the god of thinness. It is the *most obvious* panacea for the chaos that stalks her consciousness.

Those familiar with certain societies of southern Asia realize that "be virile" is one of the most powerful of all cultural suggestions that men receive. On the other hand, impotence and infertility are terrifying prospects that entail a total loss of "face" and self-respect. One's worth as a man is contingent upon being a skilled and potent sexual performer. Considerable anxiety is frequently generated by the slightest hint of sexual inadequacy. This explains the astounding lengths to which the men of these cultures will go to ensure their virility. I have myself witnessed men visiting the snake market area of Taipei, Taiwan. That is where one can obtain the concoctions that will enhance and maintain virility. These men pay good sums of money to consume snake's blood and venom, pulverized rhinoceros' horn, certain types of dried lizards, and so forth.

While there, I saw stall vendors demonstrate the supposed effectiveness of cobra venom by giving it to a large monkey. Somehow, the clever primate was then able to give itself a formidable erection which convinced the male onlookers of the venom's potency. The vendor gave some anti-venom to the monkey and assured prospective customers that he would safeguard their health by doing the same. A number of the men partook of the venom and, thanks to their ready suggestibility, looked all the better for having done so. I remained dubious about the secret sexual properties of cobra venom. However, I was totally convinced that their culture spoke to men very seriously with the message to "be virile."

People in south Asian societies also fall off the bandwagon of conventional, reality-conquering beliefs and rituals. It probably happens less often than in Western societies because their traditional belief systems are more intact and more capable of coping with even higher levels of human suggestibility. None the less, when it happens, they too focus their loose suggestibility on other prevalent cultural suggestions. Unlike weight-obsessed Western societies, however, those societies place tremendous emphasis on sexual potency and performance. Therefore, one of the monoideistic disorders that emerges there involves symptoms associated with a specific *sexual* part of the body. In this case, the monomotivation entails repetitive attempts to make the sexual organ bigger. The very same process is involved in the anorexic's equally maladaptive monomotivation to be *smaller*. In Western cultures, the "be thin" suggestion is aimed more at women than men. The reverse is true with the southern Asian "be virile" suggestion. For that reason, we see far more anorexia nervosa in women and more koro in men. Western men are increasingly coming to accept the "be thin" suggestion and the number of male anorexics is currently rising as a result. For now, south Asian women appear relatively safe from the cultural haranguing about the importance of being a great sexual performer.

Lydia Temoshok and C. Clifford Attkisson add to our understanding of disorders like anorexia nervosa as they interact with culture. They agree with Hilda Bruch when they describe anorexia nervosa as "an extreme form of adaptation to psychological gear shifting between life stages."[17] We already saw that preanorexic people are most vulnerable as they perceive their own "nothingness" and ineffectiveness in the face of an overwhelming complex set of approaching realities. But, again like Bruch, they write that only certain individuals are susceptible to the disorder. Bruch said it was the person's excessive dependence on societal opinion and judgment that caused these individuals to become fixated on slimness as an answer to all facets of their existences. Highly suggestible people are more easily conditioned to cultural suggestion. Consequently, they are more vulnerable to maladaptive "specializations" that involve these suggestions. Temoshok and Attkisson use the phrase "*externalized* sensitivity" to denote this heightened susceptibility to an uncritical adoption of cultural suggestion. They add that this entails a self-identity defect in which the boundaries between self and "nonself" become dangerously diffused.

Temoshok and Attkisson also point out that anorexia nervosa is part of a continuum of suggestibility-based disorders.[18] In keeping with what has been said so far, they describe this entire class of psychological disturbance as a "frantic search for cognitive control." Again, however, they are cognitive *biases* that should not be necessary if a culture is working to channel our suggestibility and to give us the illusion of order and control.

Well-functioning cultures have elaborate *traditional* rites of passage that normally carry us through periods of conflict and change. These usually involve cathartic *group* rituals and ceremonies that ease the anxiety that derives from life's uncertainties and difficult adjustments. One reason that Western society fails us and forces us into *private* religions and *personal* constrictions of reality is that it lacks such structure. Beyond that, its mainstay of traditional self-transcending myths has become seriously weakened in recent history. For that reason, Temoshok and Attkisson are quite right in proposing that Western society would have greater numbers of people suffering from the types of disorder that we have been describing here. In chapter 4, we saw evidence that human beings have a need for a minimum amount of reality-transcending belief. Below that, we become more susceptible to the symptoms of mental illness and, in particular, the symptoms of monoideistic disorders. Given the ragtag shape of conventional belief systems in the West, we should be more inclined to suffer from the "private" types of insanity.

## Other private religions

Volumes could be written on the miscarriage of suggestibility and the myriad of clinical symptoms that are produced when this happens. Anorexia nervosa is just one of many clinical manifestations of errant suggestibility that cannot be incorporated into conventional misrepresentations of reality. I dwelt on that particular disorder because it is such a good example of how suggestibility becomes transformed into feeble private religions when "better" conventional ideology fails to accommodate that suggestibility. Other examples, both within and outside our own culture, could be discussed as well. Some of these are culture-bound, while others are not. For those interested in other non-Western, culture-bound monoideistic disorders, let me recommend they read about the Dhat syndrome (semen anxiety), Windigo (the obsession that one will become cannibalistic), and Latah (hyper-suggestibility expressed as involuntary mimicking of others).[19] Let me now give brief mention to two other Western disorders that clearly seem to be derailments of suggestibility and the self-deception process. This is warranted since this theoretical model has important implications for the treatment of these monoideistic forms of psychopathology.

### Obsessive-compulsive neurosis

An obsession is an intrusive and unwelcomed *thought* that plagues an individual. It is highly intrusive and resists people's efforts to rid their minds of its content. On the other hand, a compulsion is a repetitive *action* which a person feels strongly compelled to act out. Great anxiety is usually experienced if the compulsion is not, or cannot, be performed. An obsession fits exactly into Kaffman's definition of a monoideism, while a compulsion is a perfect example of a monomotivation. Obsessions and compulsions very often occur together, which is why both terms are used in the disorder's label. A short case description may be helpful in showing that obsessive-compulsive neurosis is also a "private" religion.

A very pleasant woman in her early forties came to see me. She complained of an "ugly thought" from which she had suffered for over seven years. This woman claimed that every day of her life had been a living hell since that thought first invaded her world. As is typical in such cases, the harder she fought to remove the thought, the bigger and more horrific it became. Her obsession involved the persistent thought that her husband would swallow a piece of glass and that he would bleed to death as a result of stomach damage. Her compulsion was a behavior pattern that followed directly from the obsession. Each day after her husband went to work this woman took it upon herself to examine every glass, cup, plate, and saucer in her kitchen. Methodically and with great precision, she carefully ran her finger along the rims of all these breakable objects. She was looking for any signs of even the slightest nick or missing chip of glass and always managed to discover one (or imagine one). At that point, she got out the vacuum cleaner and vacuumed every inch of the house, including the curtains, drapes, and furniture. Following this exhaustive vacuum job, she would spread all the takings from the vacuum cleaner onto a clean sheet of white paper. She then spent great lengths of time going through the dirt looking for the killer chip of glass. Most of her days were consumed with this unfortunate ideation and ritual.

What makes obsessive-compulsive neurosis especially interesting is the fact that the sufferer is almost always the *last* person in the world who would want, or commit, what is contained in their obsession. They tend to be highly conforming people who have been exceptionally well conditioned to society's moral code. In fact, most have overdeveloped consciences which, I believe, dispose them to monoideisms that involve *moral* cultural taboos. These individuals are usually well above average intelligence and are a joy to work with in therapy. The only exception is that they usually do not improve. The reason for this is that they, like the anorexic, have a private religion that is serving them. It may be a clumsy religion but, like all religions, it does not let itself be taken away without an awful struggle.

Clinical psychologists have very little idea about what actually causes obsessive-compulsive neurosis. In fact, it is one of the most poorly understood of all syndromes. Unlike the recent research relating anorexia nervosa to hyper-suggestive states, almost no similar work has been done with obsessive-compulsive disorders. This is especially unfortunate given the epidemiological evidence showing a sharp increase in this disorder, especially in children. Despite the limited data on this form of mental illness, I feel confident in saying that it is another "problem of religion." Other mental health professionals, in addition to Kaffman, are beginning to consider the role that suggestibility plays in the development of psychopathology. Eugene Bliss of the University of Utah Medical School is one such person. He, like Kaffman, proposes that hyper-suggestibility and auto-hypnosis underlie obsessions and compulsions. I am confident that future quantitative investigations will bear this out.

One curious feature of obsessive-compulsive neurosis gives us a clue to the "religious" nature of that problem. This concerns the way in which *paradoxical intention* temporarily interrupts and removes the disorder. This therapy technique involves instructing the obsessive-compulsive person *not* to resist the obsessive thought. They are told to let it happen. If they ask why, they are often given some psycho-babble about the therapist needing more detail about the specific nature of the cognition. I did this with the woman in mention here. I admit that, at the time, I was at a loss to understand or treat her effectively. Paradoxical intention seemed worth a try, but I had no idea why it should work. I gave her some impressive-sounding reason for needing her to abandon herself to the thought that her husband might swallow glass and die. In fact, I told her to carry around a pencil and pad and write down the thought in vivid and explicit detail. The assignment struck her as somewhat cruel and exceedingly difficult to do. But she agreed, as she was very keen to please me just as she wanted to please everyone else in her life. One week later, she came in for her appointment in tears – tears of joy that is. Her first words were, "What did you do to me!?" She went on to say that she was *unable* to think of the awful thought for the entire week. My intuition told me that her happiness was mixed with a sense of loss. This feeling was reinforced when she stated that she wanted to stop seeing me in therapy. Termination seemed premature to me but she insisted that she was cured and canceled all future appointments. Two weeks later I received a call from her saying the ugly thought and the vacuuming had returned. We made another appointment. At the start of that session, she told me she had figured out that I had "tricked" her.

With that realization, her symptoms returned. As it happens, paradoxical intention usually works only temporarily, when it works at all.

She was right. I had tricked her. Specifically, I was able to remove a vital link in the chain of cognitions that made up the private religion that was functioning to highly *constrict* her perception of the world. Many such monoideistic symptoms derive their energy from anxiety associated with the violation of cultural taboos. All obsessions are "evil" in nature. Just as most religions have and need a devil, so did hers. By telling her to go along with the thought, I was telling her that it was not really all that bad. I was playing down the size of her devil by telling her to get to know it more. That temporarily defused her anxiety and caused a remission of her symptoms. Her mini-religion was able to reorganize itself once she had rationalized what I had done to her. Then I became a safe person again to whom she could return. For that brief period, I was unconsciously her worst enemy. Once her symptoms returned, we again related very well together. However, I had no further success with her and eventually referred her to another psychologist. I met this woman almost two years later and was saddened to learn that she was still suffering with her obsession.

It would be tempting to attribute this woman's affliction to a secret hatred of her husband. One could find logic in the explanation that she actually wanted her husband to die and be out of her life. But, as rational as that might seem, it was not the case. It almost never is with this type of person. This woman loved her husband more than most women love their husbands. She knew that. I knew that. He knew it. It would have been an amateurish and counterproductive gesture to work on the premise that she unconsciously harbored hatred for him. The same is usually true for other obsessive-compulsive individuals who imagine all sorts of horrible things happening. What they are doing is in response to a more *generalized* sense of being out of control and pitted against a chaotic world with which they cannot cope.

As Kaffman writes, there exists "the existential need of a system of beliefs that is present in all of us so as to provide us with a meaningful life and with guidelines for personal behavior."[20] This *general* need for order and a sense of direction serves as "a natural reservoir of fuel for the maintenance of the monoideistic pattern," according to Kaffman. If our suggestibility is not funneled into culturally endorsed beliefs that create the illusion of order, we have to attempt it ourselves. The obsessive-compulsive person is doing just that, albeit in an inefficient way. For some reason, culture proves unable to afford them the *absolute* madness that would prevent them from developing *clinical* madness.

It is interesting why obsessive-compulsive people take on those particular monoideistic symptoms and not others. Over the past few hundred years, we have seen a striking shift in the content of obsessive-compulsive symptoms. Prior to the breakdown of traditional religious belief systems, most clinical obsessions and compulsions revolved around religion and sex. John Bunyan, the seventeenth-century author of *Pilgrim's Progress*, reportedly had the obsessive thought that he should "sell Christ." That thought plagued him and led him to repeat "No, I will not sell him!" over and over again. In those days, religious paranormal beliefs were the one overriding method for creating order. But even that relatively solid belief occasionally failed to meet the needs of someone like John Bunyan. Still, religion was the primary cultural defense mechanism upon which people relied for self-deception. Consequently, the rare clinical obsession that did appear still took on content related to conventional religion. When that was not the case, the content tended to involve an infraction against a sexual taboo. Even that, though, came back to religion, as it was primarily religion that manufactured and upheld the sexual constraints.

Today, the most common obsessions and compulsions focus on dirt and violence. We know that people who develop obsessive-compulsive neurosis are, like the anorexic, quite methodical and order-seeking as part of their basic personality structure. Their greater need to contain the many loose ends in life probably makes them more inclined to constrict reality beyond what they would be able to do with current Western cultural fictions. Unlike in the past, the content of obsessions and compulsions rarely take a religious form. Although a sad reflection on contemporary society, themes related to contamination and violence may be foremost in many of our minds. If we in the West had a more intact traditional religious lap into which we could fall, even such order-hungry people could achieve a healthy constriction of reality. In that regard, we could again surmise that we have many more *clinically* obsessive and compulsive people than in the past or in societies with intact religious paranormal belief systems.

Freud was correct about religion to the extent that he called it an attempt to gain control over one's *sensory* world. I believe that obsessive-compulsive disorder, as well as all counter-intelligent behavior, is intended to prevent sensory overload. That was the very crux of Bergson's ideas on the evolutionary need for counter-intelligence. It is to limit the degree and nature of information that would otherwise reach our senses through "pure" intelligence. Even "healthy" religion has many obsessive and compulsive features. Religious services are group hypnosis sessions that enable people to ingest the suggestions that will determine the content of their obsession and the form of the compulsion. Hypnotists know that suggestions given under hypnosis last only a week or two in most cases. It is therefore no coincidence that church services are usually spaced out by lengths of time that enable the waking trance to be maintained. Moreover, it is much easier to achieve a trance state while part of a group. Ask any stage hypnotist, church leader, or evangelical "healer." The bigger the group, the easier it is to achieve the "common everyday trance" that enables self-transcending belief. Also, the more people engaged in collective irrationality, the less irrational, foolish, and deviant each individual feels.

However, there is a great difference between the obsessions and compulsions in conventional religion and those in obsessive-compulsive disorder. The obsessive and ritualistic elements of traditional religious practice are an aspect of the "normal" insanity referred to by Freud and Spiro. The private religion of the obsessive-compulsive neurotic is a form of clinical pathology that lacks group support and approval. Obsessive-compulsive disorder is an inefficient attempt to do independently what can only be done collectively. As a weak form of cognitive self-deception, it demands that people invest vast quantities of psychic energy in keeping their private reality contortions alive.

Despite all efforts to convince themselves of their irrational symptoms, their private distortions of reality remain verifiably false. The woman's husband could have eaten and drunk from her kitchenware till the cows came home, and he would not have died from swallowing glass. Furthermore, these people are never able to avoid feeling abnormal and less worthwhile for their private lies about the world. Again, collective self-deception is far superior to personal self-deception. The monoideistic disorders are clumsy, *independent* attempts to do what human beings were intended to do *together* – invent order with patterned self-transcending beliefs. Culture has failed the obsessive-compulsive neurotic in the same way it has failed the one with anorexia nervosa.

## Paranoia

Kaffman does a thorough job of detailing paranoia as an autosuggestive monoideistic disorder.[21] He describes it as an "internalized mythical script" in which the person becomes completely absorbed in a delusional belief. Like the other monoideistic types of psychopathology, paranoia serves to provide relief from underlying anxiety through a process of intellectual and emotional *dissociation*. Paranoia creates "rigid forced thinking with a locked up thematic content."[22] As in anorexia nervosa and obsessive-compulsive neurosis, external reality is greatly constricted and the paranoid person can hide in a highly focused, singular ideation. The paranoid does manage to avoid sensory overload and shut out external reality by distorting and reducing it to the size of the delusion.

The paranoid also employs a self-induced trance that "creates an altered state of consciousness that will selectively affect the perception of external events and modify the capacity for volitional control."[23] The auto-hypnotic process involved enables paranoid individuals to distract themseves from thoughts and perceptions that could compete with or contradict their delusional belief system. Kaffman notes that paranoid monoideisms inevitably lead people to withdraw socially. Their private religion, with its highly restrictive cognitive theme, relegates most other activities and interests to second place. According to Kaffman, this social isolation and diminished external stimulation is the perfect breeding-ground for a self-sustaining autosuggestive state.

Like the anorexic who becomes totally closed to suggestions from outside, all of the paranoid's suggestibility is directed inwards. Kaffman writes that paranoia evolves into "a state of waking trance" in which he or she can no longer recognize any logical inconsistencies in their one-dimensional belief system. Again like the anorexic, the transition from the pre-onset condition to the fully developed disorder is a dramatic one. The individual shifts from a state of excess or unchanneled suggestibility to a state of *hypo*-suggestibility, or non-suggestibility. As these people absorb their own suggestibility in constructing an altered reality, they become unrecognizable to those who knew them previously. Most lose vitality for life as well as any prior spirit of spontaneity. Their sense of humor disappears, as does most of their compassion and sympathy for others. In paranoia, as in anorexia nervosa, people often become far less sensitive to physical pain. They also tend to disregard any physical disorders that they might have. Some observers have noted that such behaviors are characteristic of altered states of consciousness, like hypnosis.[24]

Very little research has been done concerning the personality makeup of paranoid people while they are in the pre-onset condition. The same is true for the types of communication and social interaction to be found in their families of origin. It remains unclear if similar background factors also predispose the would-be paranoid to become excessively suggestible. That would be a fruitful area for future research. What does seem clear is that paranoia is another form of self-hypnosis in which the person *autosuggests* himself or herself into believing in a highly constricted version of reality.

Kaffman does help us understand why paranoids develop symptoms of paranoia rather than other types of monoideistic symptoms. The explanation may relate to the communication patterns that Kaffman observed in families that produced paranoid individuals. Kaffman writes:

> We identified a long-standing pattern of communication with their families and their surroundings characterized by stereo-typed transactions around a fixed theme, rigid rules, dogmatic beliefs, suspiciousness, and/or a very apprehensive approach to life deeply rooted in the family. . . . These repetitive family patterns of inflexible interpersonal communication with a one-sided way of looking at the world would seem to be fertile ground for paranoia.[25]

Kaffman found that such families had "inflexible belief constructs," which encouraged a perception of the world as "filled with inexorable existential dangers."[26] People reared in such an environment become exposed to this type of "script." As a result, Kaffman believes that the paranoid person has fully internalized the suggestions that were part of this mythical family communication script. The mechanisms underlying paranoia are the same as those in other monoideistic disorders. It is only the symptoms (or beliefs) that vary. Given Kaffman's observations about the families of paranoid people, it follows that the content of their private religion would center on ideations of persecution.

I said before that devils *work* like gods in that they also help the believer to create the illusion of order. The three syndromes that have been mentioned illustrate how gods and devils can be used in varying ways to save oneself, by shrinking one's understanding of the world. The paranoid's religion has no god. He or she has settled for some version of a devil that poses a threat. Most "shoulds" and "shouldn'ts" are established in relation to the devilish enemy. None the less, like all believers, they have successfully manufactured a mythical belief system and a related set of rules. Their miniscule perceptual world is more manageable and they prevent sensory overload. Kaffman writes:

> In most cases the monoideistic paranoid belief provides an *absorbing* cause to work for, a goal, and a direction in life to a person . . . whose world was lacking sufficient guidelines for one's behavior. The patient's tenacious clinging to his mono-ideistic belief gives him an *illusory* escape from his fear to a life perceived to be full of existential threats.[27]

Kaffman's keen insights include a recognition of the "religious" nature of monoideistic forms of mental illness. He writes specifically about the monoideistic transformations of the percep-tions of people who have undergone religious conversion or a cult experience:

> Pervasive indoctrination by new faiths that promise spiritual rebirth, supernal transcendence, and true happiness may induce a monoideistic state of mystical ecstasy and emotional exaltation. Something similar may occur to proselytes to certain highly structured 'growth' group experiences . . . designed to open an additional dimension of living . . . that *transcends the mind*. Persons who join these charismatic groups on a fixed and regular basis may become completely absorbed by the conviction that fundamental changes to the good have taken place in their inner worlds. They find relief by . . . *shutting off the mind from external reality*. Often the individual develops a semiautomatic thinking schema, completely absorbed by his ruminative system of belief, while feeling a new sense of being and of spiritual fulfillment.[28]

We can see that the symptoms of religion closely resemble the symptoms of monoideistic disturbances. They are both *closed* mental states utilized to repel external reality.

Three other disorders that are clearly monoideistic "private religions" are hypochondriasis, conversion disorder, and certain extreme types of phobias. I shall not discuss them here, as I believe these symptoms *work* in the same way as the other monoideisms and their monomotivations. Each enables people to *lose* themselves and constrict their perceptual worlds by auto-suggestive ahderence to highly restrictive ideation. But let me give brief mention to one disorder that appears to be – but is not – a true monoideistic psychopathology. That is multiple personality.

Eugene Bliss does an outstanding job of describing multiple personality as an auto-hypnotic disturbance preceded by hyper-suggestibility.[29] Even so, multiple personality seems to be caused in a somewhat different way from the other monoideistic disorders. I would not contest the recent research showing that people with this disorder have extremely elevated levels of suggestibility. My personal contact with a few multiple personality cases leaves me in no doubt that they are among the most suggestible of all people. However, as we also know, people with multiple personality almost always have a history of being seriously abused as children.[30] As such, I am more inclined to agree with David Spiegel's view that multiple personality is a *subtype of post-traumatic stress disorder*.[31] The fact that hyper-suggestibility is still readily apparent (i.e., not absorbed) in the fully developed condition also makes me think it operates differently from the "private religions."

In monoideistic problems, the suggestibility is tightly held in the highly focused symptoms. The remarkable way that auto-suggestion works in multiple personality remains a mystery. What makes it so different from the monoideistic disturbances is that the suggestibility remains *available*, always ready to be used in the creation of varying personalities. That "free" suggestibility accounts for the fact that the person with multiple personality disorder is usually an outstanding hypnotic subject. The "bound" suggestibility of those with true monoideistic disturbances usually makes them poor hypnotic subjects. That is, of course, ironic given the pre-onset hyper-suggestibility that is often observed. But we must remember that the monoideistic syndromes themselves make almost *complete* use of any available suggestibility. That is why it is so difficult to influence them in psychotherapy.

## Curing bad lies

I would not pretend to have the final answer on how to treat the class of psychological disorders that we have been discussing. However, our new understanding of these problems could point the direction to more effective therapies. In designing these treatment strategies, we could benefit from a look at how non-Western therapies treat monoideistic disorders. As we recall, some of the monoideistic psychopathologies in the West have direct counterparts in non-Western cultures. What many will find surprising is that "witchdoctor" therapies have a far higher success rate with monoideistic mental illness than the therapies we are now using in the West. Some cross-cultural literature on the methods of the traditional healer (as most prefer to be called) can help us understand their greater effectiveness. I had the opportunity to witness some of these approaches at first hand when I was living and teaching in Africa some years ago. I believe that some breakthroughs in the treatment of monoideistic mental disorders are possible if we can learn from the "primitive" healers in non-Western societies.

We might first look at just how ineffective our Western therapies are in curing monoideistic mental problems. They are *very* ineffective. Anorexia nervosa and obsessive-compulsive neurosis are two cases in point. Over half of those treated for anorexia nervosa derive little or no benefit whatsoever. Another 25 percent show only partial improvement. Of those treated in hospital settings, nearly half will need to be rehospitalized within two years. The statistics for obsessive-compulsive disorder are no better. Studies show that less than one-third of these people stage a complete recovery with psychotherapy. Long-term studies show that less than half have recovered after five years of treatment. These results are even more depressing when one considers that, over time, many people who suffer from psychological disorders get better *without* help. This phenomenon has been called "spontaneous recovery" by psychologists. The reasons why people sometimes improve without treatment remains unclear. But if we take the spontaneous recovery factor into account, the quoted recovery rates seem even worse. One wonders if present treatment methods are of any value to these people. Either way, it is very clear that these and other monoideistic disorders are very resistant to Western psychotherapy.

On the other hand, many cross-cultural psychologists and medical anthropologists have commented on the astonishingly high cure rates by traditional non-Western healers. Having had the chance to compare both approaches, I have no doubt that the typical "witchdoctor" is a far better agent of change than the typical Western psychologist or psychiatrist. The difference is especially great when it comes to treating "hysterical" or mono-ideistic disorders. John G. Kennedy makes this point in discussing the power and effectiveness of the Nubian Zar therapies in Ethiopia. He writes that these ceremonial treatments for mental illness are both quicker and more effective than Western psycho-therapies.[32]

The reason such non-Western therapies work better with monoideistic disorders is that they make much better use of suggestion and the patient's suggestibility. Their general success is to be expected given that these disturbances are maladaptive displacements of suggestibility. It is only logical that the therapeutic use of suggestion should be used with problems of suggestibility. The manner in which a "primitive" treatment like Nubian Zar therapy makes use of suggestion serves to highlight other important factors that maximize effectiveness. It also enables us to speculate about the relative ineffectiveness of Western psycho-therapies in treating this particular category of mental disturbance.

First, the treatment takes place with an audience, sometimes numbering as many as 50 or 100 members as in the case of Nubian Zar therapy. We saw earlier that suggestibility is heightened in group settings. The audiences at non-Western therapies are sometimes limited to the extended family, but are often open to neighbors and other non-relatives as well. The attending crowd is frequently very active and involved, thus sending the treatment session into quite an emotional pitch. The use of driving and *repetitive* sounds are almost universal to these non-Western healing techniques. This adds to the intensity of feeling that accompanies therapy, and also enhances the patient's suggestibility and facilitates the therapeutic trance that is the essential aspect of treatment.

The emotional intensity combined with repetitive auditory stimulation gives the treatment process a strong right hemisphere emphasis. This contrasts dramatically with the verbal insight-oriented "left brain therapies" common in the West. Colleen Ward, now at New Zealand's Canterbury University, has written in detail about methods of trance induction. She states that "sensory bombardment" is often an essential element of the induction process. According to Ward, the right hemisphere of the brain must be engaged in order to precipitate and maintain trance.[33] Flooding people with all types of sensory stimulation appears to assist in shifting a person into a right hemisphere mode. A good deal of other research has also demonstrated that the repetition of such rhythmic sounds and images fosters trance by engaging right hemisphere capacities.[34] These usually inhibit the dominant left hemisphere. Previously, we also saw that hypnosis and suggestibility appear to be right hemisphere phenomena. Since monoideistic disorders are states of auto-suggestion or self-hypnosis, it follows that these disturbances relate directly to right brain cognitive processes. Therefore, it is only reasonable to suspect that therapies involving right brain functions would have a better chance of dealing with monoideistic forms of psychopathology.

An increasing number of mental health professionals are, in fact, speaking of the limitations of the language-based left brain therapies that dominate in the West. They argue that many types of mental illness are, by their very nature, irrational and illogical. We are reminded of G. K. Chesterton's excellent observation from *Orthodoxy*: "the madman is not the one who has lost reason. The madman is the one who has lost everything except reason." It is as if he were speaking directly about the origin of monoideistic disorders when he wrote those words. Monoideistic types of mental disturbance are attempted flights from reason into irrationality. The irrationality represents a haven from the icy realities that would otherwise be exposed by the hand of reason. Irrationality must take over in people whose reasoning ability, or "pure" intelligence, threatens to make serious psychological trouble. As such, intellectual left brain therapies that focus on reasoning, logic and rational reflection are totally inappropriate with monoideistic disorders. They can have no beneficial impact on behavior that is completely irrational. On the other hand, Ari Kiev speaks of the high degree of "magic" built into non-Western therapies and how they are primarily "nonrational attempts to deal with nonrational forces."[35] Western therapies lack not only vitality but also the "magic" that is necessary to make an effective assault on wayward forms of irrationality.

There are other components of non-Western healing that make it a more effective method by which to treat derailed suggestibility. One of them has to do with the social status of the patient.

Mentally disturbed people have a much higher social status in many non-Western societies. Their illness is often considered a special endowment from supernatural sources. The disease itself is frequently given special attention, as it may encode a message from a spirit or god. This is evident in the way that the patient is sometimes presented to the healer. For example, the Nubians dress female patients to look like a bride. She is heavily perfumed and decorated with henna and kohl. Many such symbols of purification are employed, for male and female patients alike. The special regard for the mentally sick can also be seen in the many cultures in which mentally ill people are themselves elevated to the status of healer. Short of that, it is safe to say that the patient in non-Western cultures has the benefit of group support and a collective embrace.

Despite some increased tolerance toward the psychologically disturbed in the West, we still attach an ugly stigma to mental illness. This fuels feelings of social isolation and causes the mentally ill to feel less a part of their cultural group. Such conditions hamper therapeutic efforts in the West. However, by gathering around the afflicted person and making a great fuss of him or her, the non-Western patient is prepared for a return to the mainstream of culture. The person often responds to this welcoming ritual and it becomes easier for the healer to help the person return to majority behavior. Their "private religion" can be replaced by the healthier absolute insanity of culturally sanctioned ideology.

The status of the healer in many non-Western therapies also accounts for the greater success with autosuggestive types of mental disturbance. He or she is generally given a special *public* place in the minds of all people in the society. An elaborate and highly ritualistic *public* initiation often serves to establish the therapeutic role of the healer. Frequently, the healer is fantastically adorned and given possession of the "magical" instruments that will aid in the healing process. The first "cures" are often public and involve many clear displays of the healer's curative powers. An air of awe and excitement is created at initiations as well as at each treatment session. The sense of mystery is enhanced by the endless rituals carried out by the highly respected healer.

All this leads to a conviction by everyone, including the patient, that the healer can indeed heal. The patient *knows* the treatment will work. John G. Kennedy writes that, by the time the non-Western patient enters treatment, he or she knows that "this is it!" That is, the patient is fully certain of the healer's legitimacy and of the treatment's effectiveness. The patients are nearly cured before the therapy begins. There is little chance of failure. Kennedy adds that the intellectual and rational therapies in the West are highly artificial and contrived by comparison. We in Western society are totally unable to fool and brainwash potential patients to such an extent. We patients enter therapy with knees knocking. We usually lack as much confidence in our therapist and the therapy as we lack in ourselves. The unassuming therapists who appear before us look so unimpressive, diminished, and ordinary. On the other hand, non-Western healers are very assuming. They assume that they can cure you! The patient assumes so too. Such trust and conviction greatly facilitate treatment. The unabashed commercial aspect of Western therapies makes the patient feel more like a customer, and a cheated one at that. How does one heal (or in this case *convert*) alienated, distrusting customers? Not easily! That is why we Western psychologists are so inept with auto-hypnotic monoideistic disorders.

A word or two about the actual elements of non-Western therapies may also help us understand their high success rate with problems of untracked suggestibility. The vast majority employ deep trance. In many of the non-Western therapy ceremonies, the healer goes into trance with the patient. The Curandero, or healer, of northern Peru does this using a mescaline-containing cactus as a catalyst for the mutual trance state. The trance used by traditional healers is not unlike what we have been calling hypnosis, except that it is a much more supercharged and potent variety. Ritualistic practices abound and set the atmosphere in most non-Western treatment sessions. The healer creates what Kennedy calls an "altered ritually-constructed world" for the patient. Rituals combine with the repetitive noises, music, and activities of the audience to increase the patient's suggestibility to a workable level. A full-scale Nubian Zar treatment, for example, goes from early morning to evening, and lasts for seven days. The drama is intense and the activity fast. The continual use of a spell-inducing ritual culminates with an animal sacrifice on the seventh day. This might involve a chicken or pair of pigeons if the family is poor. A sheep or lamb would be sacrificed if the family could afford it. The animal is slaughtered above the patient and the blood is allowed to drip over the patient's face. The blood is smeared over the entire face and body.

Then some blood is mixed with henna, cloves, and water. And the patient drinks this potion. Throughout the seven days of Nubian Zar therapy, the patient moves in and out of trance many times. The dissociative trance states are often accompanied by great trembling fits that can be removed by certain rituals and songs that the healer performs. As one can imagine, everyone is near exhaustion by the end of this type of treatment. Still, in the majority of cases the patient's symptoms have lifted by the end of it all. Why?

We need to keep in mind that those with monoideistic disturbances have pinned their suggestibility onto maladaptive constrictions of reality. In the course of insulating themselves with their auto-hypnotic symptoms, they become closed off and far less suggestible than an ordinary person. The therapist must treat suggestibility-based problems in a person who lacks available suggestibility. The patient is already in a deeper trance than the "waking trance" of the ordinary person. Their suggestibility is already tied up in the service of their symptoms, which makes them poor hypnotic subjects. The job of the therapist is to free the person's suggestibility. Then he or she must attach it to more workable socially sanctioned distortions of reality.

But, how is it possible to plant alternative suggestions in a patient if the patient is not open to suggestion? The non-Western healer knows the answer. It is force! You pull out all stops and do everything that will draw out the person's locked up suggestibility. Everything done in treatments such as Nubian Zar therapy is intended to generate suggestibility. Another more powerful trance is superimposed over the patient's autosuggestive trance. The relentless pounding of drums, the active audience, the continuous string of colorful rituals, the awesome presence of a *convincing* healer, the ebullient touching and social attention – all these together create a deep, *externally*-induced trance which displaces the patient's personal one. The electricity generated at many of these healing sessions is beyond the imagination of most Westerners. The constant drumming alone is enough to send almost anyone into a trance given enough time. Aldous Huxley writes about this trance-inducing quality of drumming in *The Devils of London*:

No man, however highly civilized, can listen for very long to African drumming, or Indian chanting, or Welsh hymn-singing, and retain his critical and self-conscious personality . . . if exposed long enough to the tom-toms and the singing, every one of our philosophers would end up by capering and howling with the savages.[36]

Wolfgang Jilek writes that non-Western healing may be best understood as therapeutic *brainwashing*.[37] The altered state of consciousness they produce in the patient makes them ripe to have their assumptive worlds reconstructed. The techniques maximize the chances of success by creating in the patient a hyper-suggestive state of total irrationality. Non-Western treatments virtually eliminate left brain faculties from the therapeutic process. The patient is powerless to fight back with logic. The force and dynamism of their suggestibility-enhancing methods enable them to break all "suggestibility resistance" (a phrase used by Elizabeth Loftus of the University of Washington). In so doing, they *detach* the person's suggestibility from the symptoms to which it was bound.

So, what should Western therapists do differently to treat monoideistic disorders? Very few of us would consider butchering chickens or sheep on our nice office carpets. Not many would want to spend up to seven days in the intensive treatment of a single patient. Only the most sporting of us would even consider donning a spectacular costume and dancing or chanting in the presence of our clientele. As for bathing our customers in henna, kohl, and cloves – well you can forget that too. Beyond that, I am not sure if many paying patients would look favorably upon those sorts of antics. No. Even though many patients would delight in the sight of such a "coming out" on the part of their formal Western therapist, that is not the answer. As Vijoy Varma stresses, the therapist must take into account the "socio-cultural reality" in which they are operating.[38] Still, we have learned some very important things from the non-Western treatments. They tell us that it is possible to help those who suffer from auto-hypnotic disorders. We also know it is necessary to treat the disorder with hypnosis or trance. Additionally, they teach us that this can be done by overpowering any suggestibility resistance that exists as a result of their *private* trance (i.e., their monoideistic syndrome). We see that with enough heightening of suggestibility, it is possible to gain *external* control of the patient and of his or her internalized suggestibility. So, the challenge for the Western therapist is one of *how* to elevate sufficiently the suggestibility of people in the autosuggestive grips of monoideistic disturbances.

Unfortunately, the typical Western therapy approach is, at all levels, lacking the necessary structure and methods by which to bring about what is essentially a religious conversion. Although hypnosis is the logical treatment strategy for monoideistic disorders, the Western brand of hypnosis pales in comparison to the dramatic inductions achieved by non-Western healers. Most of the external suggestibility-enhancing aids that we have mentioned are absent. Regardless, the direct adoption of non-Western therapy strategies would not work, as one would be disregarding "socio-cultural reality."

We are probably going to find that we must duplicate the "witchdoctor" treatments, but with magic of a Western variety. One might consider the use of certain selected aspects of non-Western therapies that could help us elevate the patient's level of suggestibility. One possibility would be to conduct treatment with an audience. Even that, however, would prove a logistical nightmare given the brief 50-minute treatment sessions used in the West. As "busy" as most of us seem to be in our society, it would even be a problem bringing together the extended family on a regular basis. Also, beating drums and rhythmic chanting may work in certain cultural settings, but that strategy would do very little for the Western therapist. Therefore, the Western mental health professionals are in a very difficult position. They do not have the techniques, cultural setting or charisma to "force" the patients out of their auto-hypnotic symptoms. Still, that is what they must do.

The only existing Western "therapy" that approximates a potentially effective treatment for monoideistic disorders is the type of *deprogramming* used to reclaim victims of religious brainwashing. As stated, monoideistic disorders are problems of religion. They only differ from other types of religious brainwashing in that the suggestions are *self-delivered* and culturally "clumsy." The person who succumbs to the brainwashing of one of the many small quasi-religious sects one sees today has his or her brain "washed" from an *external* source. The state of self-hypnosis of the anorexic or paranoid person is done without direct intervention from these outside agents. Even so, the therapist's challenge is the same. How does one deprogram a brainwashed person? It comes back to the use of suggestion in a way *forceful* enough to replace deviant suggestions with an alternative set of suggestions. Ideally, the new set of suggestions should bring the person closer to mainstream cultural misperceptions of reality.

As a treatment approach, deprogramming remains shrouded in mystery. The principles involved are poorly understood and ill-defined. As sociologist James Richardson writes, it also has a deservedly bad reputation.[39] Numerous reports have surfaced about kidnappings in which the abducted person is locked up in a motel room for days and terrorized without mercy during the brainwashing procedure. The deprogrammers often work in teams to "bomb," as they sometimes call it, the patient with suggestions that contradict the suggestions at the core of their brainwashing. They sometimes claim that this bombing is necessary to counteract the barrage of suggestions that the person received from their original brainwashers. The reasoning behind deprogramming is sound, but the actual practice is an unpleasant experience for all involved. Apparently, many of the deprogrammers were themselves deprogrammed at one time. Some harbor highly negative feelings concerning their earlier brainwashing conversion, and a number show surprisingly little sympathy for other victims of cult religion. Additionally, the techniques are not standardized and many deprogrammers fly by the seat of their therapeutic pants.

Some concerned and responsible individuals have proposed less coersive deprogramming techniques. Even so, such strategies should be used with great caution. They stand to do additional damage to people who are already in a precarious psychological state. Still, I believe reputable social scientists should analyze deprogramming techniques in an effort to extract any elements that could be applied to the treatment of monoideistic disorders. What we need is a more positive form of deprogramming. We must find a way to increase suggestibility and implant alternative suggestions in these people without the risk of being counterproductive in our efforts.

H. B. Hafeiz, in the *British Journal of Psychiatry*, reported a somewhat more benign method of "forcing" an elevation of suggestibility in patients with monoideistic disturbances.[40] It is worth mentioning because the technique also points out potential pitfalls in treating "problems of religion." Hafeiz reports on his work with patients suffering from hysterical conversion – a form of monoideistic mental illness that involves the loss of physical functioning in the absence of any real physical dysfunction. In this disorder, the victim constricts their perceptual world by focusing their cognitions onto the illusion that something is wrong with their body. Some of his patients were "hysterically" deaf or blind, while others had paralyzed limbs, seizures, speech disturbances, and so forth. In no cases could the symptoms be attributed to physiological irregularities. After eliciting the cooperation of his patients, Hafeiz used a combination of drugs (sodium amylobarbitone and methylamphetamine) and an electronic sleep-inducing device (Somlec) in order to elevate suggestibility. Hafeiz justified the extent of his treatment measures on the basis of the low success rate with traditional therapies.

Once his subjects were in a receptive state of hyper-suggestibility, he bombarded them with suggestions that their symptoms would disappear. What is remarkable about Hafeiz's approach is that *all* of the 61 hysterical conversion patients were treated effectively in this manner. Even though 12 of those subjects had relapsed when followed up one year later, such a success rate is extremely rare with monoideistic disturbances, or any other form of mental illness for that matter. Despite the 20 percent relapse rate, Hafeiz recommends that other mental health professionals look very closely at this form of "treatment by suggestion," as he calls it. I must admit that I cringe at the thought of using drugs artificially to enhance suggestibility levels. Still, I supppose one could argue that it is almost impossible to gain access to the tightly-held suggestibility that one sees in those with auto-suggestive syndromes. Even so, some of Hafeiz's clinical observations give cause for concern.

Hafeiz writes that the patients typically experienced great distress as their symptoms were being removed with this suggestion treatment. He reports that there were many emotional scenes with patients crying and trembling as their symptoms were being "suggested away." This is to be expected if, as I have said, such symptoms insulate these individuals from excessive exposure to reality. Their symptoms are constructed with suggestibility, in much the same way that religion and all paranormal self-deception is formed. To remove their symptoms is to steal away their "sick" religions. While these maladaptive mini-religions are themselves a source of suffering for these people, it is what they are relying upon to keep them at a safe distance from what they do not want to see or know. This leads to the question I raised earlier. What does a therapist do with a hyper-suggestible person whose "religious" symptoms have been taken away?

It is clear what one should *not* do. One should not remove monoideistic symptoms in isolation from a belief-set that can serve as a substitute for their symptoms. That is probably why

Hafeiz found that some of his patients had returned to their symptoms. It is also probable that these people turn to other clinical monoideisms to take the place of their original ones. Hafeiz reported that "symptom substitution" of this sort was minimal. However, given the relapse of some patients and the lack of long-term follow-up, one must suspect that symptom substitution took place in numerous cases. That would be anticipated if these types of disorders are *purposeful* in nature, as I am sure they are.

I believe the "witchdoctor" escapes this problem. From the little that is written on the subject, the cures of the traditional healer are permanent in most cases. The reason is that they are operating in an intact culture that has *workable* belief systems. Moreover, the patient in treatment is richly surrounded by traditional culture in the form of the audience and the endless range of cultural practices and rituals. The non-Western patient can slide more easily from their unhealthy form of counter-intelligence to the culturally sanctioned forms of counter-intelligence. The Western patient is much less apt to become nestled back into mainstream cultural distortions of reality. This is again because traditional Western cultural belief systems are no longer able to insulate many of us from the beast we are calling reality. Therefore, the Western patient is much more likely to show symptom substitution than the non-Western patient.

Traditional religion would be the most obvious healthy "fetish" to take the place of the failed religion of the Western patient. In that respect, the fanatical priest or minister is the preferred type of therapist for the person with monoideistic "problems of religion." That odd conclusion makes even more sense in light of the fact that a fairly high percentage of Western psychologists are non-believers in traditional ideological systems. Although there are many exceptions, they also tend to be somewhat counter-culture in their own perceptions of the world. These factors are reflected in the high rates of mental illness and suicide among Western psychologists and psychiatrists. As a result, Western psychotherapists are among the last people one would want to have treating monoideistic disorders. Even worse, they are still very much mired in the "do your own thing" mentality that permeates the philosophy of Western psychotherapy. People with monoideistic disorders turn to their symptoms precisely because they cannot cope independently in the face of the realities that surround them.

The person with a monoideistic disturbance is searching for an ideological footing that will create guidelines for living. To tell them to get in touch with themselves and "do their own thing" is to set them adrift without even their symptoms to keep them afloat psychologically. Therapy truly does then become a "confession without absolution." The only way to "absolve" a monoideistic disorder is to find a new home for their suggestibility. That must come in the form of a culturally sanctioned set of cognitive distortions that can provide the person with *absolute* insanity and *healthy* self-deception. Rank recognizes this when he writes that the cure for neurosis is "*legitimate* foolishness."[41] Neurosis, and in particular monoideistic neurosis, is failed "foolishness." It is also "illegitimate" foolishness because it does not represent what Becker called a "protective *collective* ideology."[42] Insight and the truth would only promote the hyper-consciousness that topples illusion. Rank was right to call Western therapy a "negative and disintegrating ideology." It is an ideological wasteland that affords insufficient prospects for self-forgetting.

So where does that leave us Western therapists? We lack most of what it takes to elevate and temporarily free the bound suggestibility of the person with a monoideistic disorder. We may be able to accomplish this artificially with drugs and technical aids. But, having done that, we are at a loss to offer people a collective "first-rate religion" to replace the symptoms. One could argue that *no* system of belief in Western society can effectively meet our self-deception needs. Fromm sees Western society as completely incapable of offering us the self-transcendence we need in order to achieve mental health. In *Escape from Freedom*, he writes that "we can't make people sane by making them adjust to this [Western] society – *we need a society that is adjusted to the needs of people*." That is so true. Disintegrating culture and disappearing *collective* foolishness are at the heart of the types of mental disturbance we have been describing here. That being the case, the Western therapist is fighting a losing uphill battle. The most he or she could then offer these lost souls is more *private* foolishness, if they can even do that. Fromm may be correct in saying that our culture has to change first. But until we somehow realize Fromm's dream of a sane society, we must do what we can in our terminally ill one.

On a more uplifting note, there have been some interesting breakthroughs in areas that could relate to the treatment of monoideistic disorders. Conceivably, these could form the basis of some new suggestibility-based therapies. They would not need to include drugs or coersive measures. For example, David Engstrom and his associates have shown that suggestibility and hypnotic susceptibility can be increased with electroencephalography (EEG) biofeedback.[43] With this technique, people are connected to a biofeedback machine that gives the person continuous information regarding the amount of alpha waves being generated by the brain. Alpha waves are associated with deep relaxation and are the dominant brain waves in hypnotic-like states. These researchers demonstrated that such alpha biofeedback training can raise hypnotic susceptibility. That would be very useful in treating hypo-suggestible people with monoideistic disorders.

Even more dramatic increases in suggestibility have been reported by Donald Gorassini and Nicholas Spanos at Carleton University in Canada.[44] Their approach aims at developing the "social-cognitive skills" that enable non-suggestible people to follow external suggestions. Gorassini and Spanos coach their subjects and allow them to observe others responding to suggestions. They even get these people to practise carrying out suggestions in a "make-believe" manner. Promising therapeutic applications should ensue from the remarkable increases in suggestibility that these researchers can produce in non-suggestible people. We saw, for example, that many victims of anorexia nervosa are inaccessibly non-suggestible once ensnared in the symptoms of that disorder. We could greatly increase our chances of success with that and other monoideistic disturbances if we have a means to open these people up to healthier alternative suggestions. The added benefit of these suggestibility-enhancing techniques is that they could be tailored into less intrusive treatments than those associated with brainwashing or deprogramming.

The problem will always remain for Western therapists that they have very little to offer patients in exchange for their monoideistic symptoms. There are no Western lies about reality that serve us effectively. Even traditional religion is being exposed as a dying fiction. It may be true, as Thornton Wilder writes in his essay, *Culture in a Democracy*, that "the world is still full of sweet and comforting lies." But, where are they? I am more inclined to side with Becker who points to a sparsity of *convincing* cultural illusions. As our opportunities for magical translations of reality disappear, we shall have ever greater numbers of monoideistic disorders. We shall also witness the continued proliferation of the desperate attempts at pseudo-religion that we see around us today in Western society.

One meager consolation is that people with failed private religions are probably less dangerous than those who have bought into culturally patterned ones. If we were all *clinically* insane, we might be more safe from each other. It is, as we saw, *absolute* insanity that we should fear most. On that discordant note, I can again put on my Grim Reaper hat.

# 7 The Unthinkable Edge

In *Endgame*, Samuel Beckett comments that "you're on earth, there's no cure for that!"[1] Most of what has been said so far seems to come down to that problematic fact.

Let us look at all the contradictions and paradoxes we have so far encountered in trying to track down the enemy in ourselves. We saw that we became the most intelligent of animals by evolving a parallel ability to be uniquely unintelligent. We genius earthworms dealt with expanding consciousness by developing the capacity to move about in a waking trance. We bought our rationality at the price of irrationality. We would come to love Truth but be driven to defeat it whenever possible. We achieved "cheerfulness" and emotional well-being by remaining absolutely insane robots driven to believe the unbelievable. We could deal with reality only by transcending it. Paranormal believing saved our species but now has us at the top of the endangered species list. Our species would kill to live and kill to love. The "healthiest" type of collective paranormal belief would foster the traits that threaten us most. Culture became the guardian of our self-deceptions, but also the murderous god of health that would enslave us to its fickle nonsense. We have used our big befogged brain to advance technology that both maximizes and minimizes our chances of survival. Now I add to that by turning from a discussion of how we can better alleviate individual suffering to a discussion of how we are all heading for oblivion. Oh, indeed, what a tangle!

Earlier, I put forward the woeful case that the formerly useful paranormal belief adaptation became a disadvantage once we entered the nuclear age. I hope I was able to show that there is a very negative side to collective paranormal self-deception, the worst aspect being the destructiveness that stems from self-transcendence. I tried to demonstrate that what was once an exercise in self-preservation may now be an exercise in self-extermination. Dobzhansky expressed his fears that our evolutionary-based refusal to accept our "fragmentariness" and nothingness has become an invitation to biological disaster. We may have arrived at the beginning of the end of our species. Still worse, it may be too late for us to readapt before our deadly technology makes its final clash with our instinct to escape reality.

As Richard Gelwick writes in his essay *Post-Critical Belief*, we may be witnessing what Sartre described as "the liquidation of the human species by the cruel enemy who has sought to destroy him . . . that hairless, evil, flesh-eating beast – man himself."[2] Gelwick ponders the prospect of a future for our species and says that "it is the revelation of Homo Sapiens' *inhumanity to humanity* that makes us wonder if humanity can prevail." He also states that the commonly held proposition that we will always prevail may turn out to be a false one. Gelwick doubts seriously our ability to meet the challenge of eradicating what underlies our inhumanity to each other. I share those reservations. I have pointed the finger at self-transcending belief as the deepest source of our destructive and suicidal natures. In my view, the very capacity that has given rise to the human animal will be what takes it down. The face of the Grim Reaper has finally been revealed as our own. Our cherished fictions about life have transformed themselves into our executioners. We are at an evolutionary cul-de-sac, a point of biological checkmate. And we will not be missed by creation: that idiot that will go on laughing in our absence. In fact, all of nature will probably breathe a big sigh of relief when the cheerful robots depart with what will surely be a huge bang.

In moments of existential zeal, some of us might deem it more honorable to die, or become crazed, with honesty than to go on deceiving ourselves. Still, given the choice, I am sure most of us would opt to remain befogged with false hope than to live and die in honesty. It is simply too much to ask that we children of the paranormal wake up in defiance of our long biological heritage and transform ourselves into mature citizens of the real world. Yes Beckett, nothing is more real than Nothing! To see what is real is to see an enormous chaotic Nothing. To see ourselves against the background of reality is to see more of the same. That is too real for a creature that is distinguished from others by intelligence and vision that is matched with equal amounts of destructive "stupidity" and blindness. The essential point to be made here is that our spirituality as well as our grotesqueness, is intimately linked to our biologies. That makes the prospect of change, and of survival, a very difficult one.

In a brilliant passage from *Herzog*, Bellow's Herzog asks what is probably the most important question at this crucial time in history: "Is the human being able to live in an inspired condition, . . . to release itself from servile dumbness, . . . to know the truth, to love another, to *consummate existence*, to abide with death in clarity of consciousness, . . . to live with *belief based on reason*?" I fear that the answer is no. This is despite the fact that the prospect of total and complete self-annihilation is *real*. In escaping the terror that would accompany a full acceptance of our conditions, we mad geniuses are inviting a highly sophisticated technological terror that could thrust the worst of all possible realities upon us. The possibility of a total nuclear eclipse of every single human worm-god (Becker's term) is no longer just an abstraction.

We always return to Kierkegaard's principal question concerning our betrayal of the truth, and our rebellion against existence. Why is it that we let loose of reality and allow falsehoods and trivia to triumph? Kierkegaard realized that the human animal remains a "restless spirit" until it forges its own forgetfulness in *self-created* trivia, distractions and faith in the *unreal*.[3] But Kierkegaard also saw the problem that this strongest human passion makes us into shackled slaves within our self-fashioned prisons. As slaves to untruth, we secretly harbor what he termed in *The Sickness Unto Death*, a "demoniac rage," the restrained rage that all slaves must struggle to contain. And maybe it is that suppressed rage that amplifies and exaggerates the cruelty that we show once we have successfully rejected earthly limitation.

There is an awful irony to our story. On one level it seems that, by rising above the nightmare of creation and the hellish orchestra of striking teeth, we would somehow have more feeling and compassion for each other. But what superficially appears to be love and caring for our own kind are mocked by the ever-recurring acts of heartlessness to which we seem so strongly drawn.

The waking trance in which we cheerful robots languish is a biologically-based mental numbness born of counter-intelligence. The partial retreat from reality that certain thinkers see as the resolution to the problem of excess intelligence is the same absolute insanity that safeguards mental health, but also locks us into the prison of belief. It is inside our prison home where the only truly senseless and purposeless destruction and killing take place. The irony shows itself so plainly when we realize that we, in our reality-transcendence, have become *worse* than the rest of creation. Still, we gained that twisted fate from the evolutionary process.

I am pessimistic about our future. I doubt that we are capable of overthrowing a biological imperative in favor of living with reality. I see clearly the suicidal impulses of our species as they are manifested in old and new efforts to transcend reality. I feel it is on a deep level that the human animal yearns for the cognitive satisfaction that life is or could be something more, or less, or somehow different from what reaches our "pure" intellect. The human brain is perfectly designed for *faith*, for a cloudy existence amidst the impossibilities we prefer to real human possibility. We were never intended "to see the skull beneath the skin," as poor Webster did in T.S. Eliot's *Whispers of Immortality*. We seem more willing to take each other's heads than we are to look beneath the surface of our self-deceptions.

Allow me to contradict myself for a final time. It is probable that certain people can live with less than optimal amounts of illusion. We saw earlier that such tenacious people are more prone toward symptoms of psychological disturbance. None the less, some do seem to develop an adverse reaction to self-deception. Becker diagnosed this as an "ulcerous gnawing" that can sometimes spring from one's knowledge that one is a "safe slave." He admitted that, to certain "strong people," this may become intolerable to the extent that they fail to obtain the intended "universal distortion of reality." Becker believed that some of these "strong" people break away from their prisons through suicide. Others he saw "drowning themselves desperately in the world." Herzog is a classic example of a person who tempts madness and treads the dangerous waters of reality. In a moment of self-reflection, Herzog understands the source of his pain: "My suffering . . . has been a mere extended form of life, a striving for *true wakefulness* and an antidote to illusion . . . "[4]

Let me personify evolution again and say that evolution did not intend for us to experience fully true wakefulness or, for that matter, life. Despite the few strong adventurers who battle on with neurotic partial wakefulness, the rest of us have no antidote to illusion. Life is truly a problem of courage. But, the vast majority of us still suffer a bad case of life cowardice. As a consequence, I believe we are destined to live with the murderous god that history will show was the giver and taker of our species. We show few signs that we are ready to rely upon, and believe in, *ourselves*. I predict we shall remain traitors to earthly truths until we destroy the very lives we want to save and prolong. Another reason I say that we are not ready to live with reality involves the unbelievably desperate lengths to which people are going today in finding a "god" to replace the crumbling traditional illusions offered by Western culture. Over the past couple of decades, we have seen an explosion of unimaginably ridiculous belief systems. We have witnessed thousands and thousands of people abandoning themselves to "gods" that should insult the intelligence of life-forms far more primitive than our own. As I look at all this degrading "religious" buffoonery, I wonder how some of us can salvage any semblance of integrity and self-respect. Surely, Rank was right in saying that we naturally gravitate toward "stupidity" in an attempt to avoid an overdose of reality. But it seems that there would be some limit to the amount of stupidity we would allow ourselves. Beyond a certain point of nonsense, it seems one would rebel and declare that they would rather starve in the void than feed themselves on such unsavory idiocy. But no. It seems that an ever-growing number of people today will take their counter-intelligence in any form, from any place. This trend alone makes me even more convinced that reality refusal is an *irrepressible* human drive and that we will continue to seek it in any form and *at any cost*.

Michael Scott Cain refers to the present scattering of paranormal belief as "psychic surrender" and says it has reached alarming proportions.[5] It is a "creeping paralysis" in which people end up abdicating life itself. He speaks of this malady as a type of spiritual zombieism that is becoming progressively widespread in the aftermath of waning conventional religious paranormal belief systems. Cain writes that psychic surrender includes born-again Christianity and its many new radical perceptions of God. However, it also encompasses the endless assortment of earthly nonsense, as well as the earthly guru-gods that lead their disciples into blissful darkness and profound stupidity. The "New Age" zombie is taking refuge in glaringly transparent quasi-religions. These take the form of everything from pop therapies and guru worship to channeling, electro-evangelism, crank metaphysics, "growth" groups, psychic healers, psychic predictors, occult advisors, seance consultations, and bizarre sects and cults of every description and persuasion.

Do you lack sex appeal? Cain directs you to the book *The Magic of Ishtar Power*:

> We must recognize that sexual attractiveness may seem to start with the physical, but a good 80 percent of it comes into play with the subtle, often subliminal, energy field that is generally called your aura. When your aura is giving off the special Ishtar Charismatic Energy, literally everyone who comes within ten feet of you will feel titillated, excited, and indeed 'turned on' about you.[6]

Do some people actually believe that? Yes! Did you say you were in need of money or a career improvement? Sardonically, Cain refers you to the book *Telecult Power*:

> Many a low-paid worker has risen to great wealth simply by 'tuning in' on the mind of his bosses and supervisors with Telecult Power. Taking an example from my experience, I was able to double my salary and get rapid promotions with practically no effort at all, simply by tuning in on my bosses' minds . . . [7]

Do such books sell? Believe it or not, they do! So, what is happening? We are witnessing desperate and disorganized attempts to achieve the illusion of magic which our culture is failing to give us. Since they are disorganized and without general consensus, most are not "healthy" types of self-deception. On the surface it may appear to be people's search to elevate consciousness and develop their "spiritual" selves. On the contrary, they represent a search for the blindness upon which we thrive. The practices are pitiful efforts to constrict one's perceptual worlds and to retreat into inferior fetishes. Furthermore, these beliefs and related rituals are ineffective to the point that they *work* no better than *clinical* insanity. They are not even worthy of being called *absolute* insanity.

Western culture is largely to blame. It has not been performing well at its principal task of focusing our natural suggestibility into collective illusion. Its gods are not working and its people are beginning to run amok in the most diabolical and self-mortifying ways. What was once a useful denial of reality has become nothing short of a discarding of life or what Cain calls "symbolic suicide." We are seeing the disappearance of the former "leaps of faith" that took us to a "healthy," albeit evil-producing, second reality. We are coming to see ungainly leaps of nonsense taken by hordes of modern spiritual cadavers who beg for amnesia. We seem willing to believe almost anything in an effort to find this. The difficulty in obtaining "healthy" conventional reality-transcending beliefs has led many of us to seek out terribly ineffective earth-bound lies. This can be seen in the form of the relatively new god that has taken the throne in Western society – *Having*. That god has grown in size to help fill the void left by the collapse of better systems of self-deception. One even sees that the god of Having has incorporated itself into traditional religious circles. Some of the more visible religious leaders are business people in every sense of the word. They exploit the religious instinct of today's lost souls. People "buy" the suggestion that money is the answer along with the one that God is the answer. In America, which is capitalism's dead end, people are even losing the distinction between the Christian God and money. The two gods have become intertwined and are fusing into one. Very few seem bothered by the antithetical philosophies underlying the two.

Money and Having have certainly taken on increasingly magical properties over the past century. Shopping malls and banks may be the sacred temples of future generations. But earlier we spoke of "good" versus "bad" forms of reality distortion and self-deception. The illusion that enough money and consumption can positively change reality is one of the *worst* illusions that we have created. It is verifiably false. I heard an interview with the author Henry Miller on his 79th birthday. He said, "You know, in all my years in America, I've never seen a *truly* rich or a *truly* happy person." You will not find many "rich" Havers, nor many happy people in a land with such obviously false gods. Again, a good illusion should not be falsifiable. In that respect, Having is probably the least convincing and most ineffective of all illusions.

In *Escape from Evil*, Becker pinpoints consumerism as one of the main "second-rate religions" in which people take refuge in contemporary society. His low regard for that "hero system" can be seen when he writes, "today we are living with the grotesque spectacle of unrestrained material production. This is perhaps the greatest and most pervasive evil to have emerged in all of history, and it may even defeat all of mankind."[8] Like Fromm, Becker saw the god of Having as an inferior type of retreat from reality. In his wisdom, he also perceived that psychotherapy is such a growing vogue today because people are desperate to find out why they are finding no peace and happiness in hedonism and Having. In the visionary conclusion to his classic book *Crowds and Power*, Elias Canetti speaks of the decline of the destructive "religions of lament." But faith never dies. Canetti describes how human beings are increasingly becoming disciples to materialism and consumerism, and to the god of More. He points out the shift that faith and belief have taken in our century: "If there is now one faith, it is faith in *production*, the modern frenzy of *increase*; and all people of the world are succumbing to it one after another."[9]

Becker reveals a general disgust at the manner in which we soak up even the most flawed cultural illusions about reality. He gives a possible explanation: "society goes on because of a silent accord by the majority that they *prefer structure to chaos*, and are willing to be lulled to sleep because of the security and ease it offers them."[10]

Fromm also regarded the West's obsession with Having as a symptom of a failed culture, and a deteriorating system of self-transcending myths. Fromm traces our present dilemma to the "death of God" development that took place in the previous century. The devastating effect this had on us is reflected in his comment from *Values, Psychology and Human Existence*, "the nineteenth century said *God is dead*; the twentieth century could say *Man is dead*."[11] Fromm also observed how we have replaced a devotion to workable heavenly gods with a deadening devotion to the god of Having. He writes:

> Means have been transformed into ends, the production and consumption of things has become the aim of life, to which living is subordinated. We produce things that act like men and men that act like things. Man has transformed himself into a thing and *worships* the products of his own hands; he is alienated from himself and has regressed to idolatry, even though he uses God's name.[12]

Fromm correctly acknowledges that, by our very nature, we need to invent "answers" that give us a sense of orientation and order. But he too writes that there are "good" and "bad" answers. This is very important because "The difference between the various answers is the difference between mental health and mental sickness, between suffering and joy, between stagnation and growth, between life and death, between good and evil."[13] In Fromm's thinking, the reason we find ourselves "dead" is because we worship an evil surrogate god, the god of Having. We have become "marketing characters" with the motto "I am as you desire me to be." We sell ourselves cheaply to anyone promoting the illusion that Having is the basis upon which to understand the world and our place in it. One additional problem with the illusion of Having is that it has made its way into our *collective* consciousness. This makes Having worse than Satanism, the Moonies, Ishtar, and Telecult power, and all the other fringe ideologies that have sprung up. As we saw, human beings are more likely to become destructive when they endorse collective self-transcending beliefs, such as traditional religious ones. In that regard, people on the cultural fringes of belief are less dangerous than those who define themselves according to mainstream cultural ideologies. Unlike the fringe believers, we Havers would probably march off to a "holy" war in defense of that popular god. That would be an interesting war: dead people marching off to battle!

It is a sad testament to our society that Having has become such a dominant cultural suggestion that some people are developing monoideistic disorders around that theme. Increasingly, clinical psychologists are encountering people who are suffering from *compulsive spending*. Like most other monoideistic disorders, the victims constrict reality into a singular ideation and a singular motivation. The result is a degrading addiction in which people need to buy and buy increasing amounts of *anything* in order to maintain their "high." That "high" is undoubtedly the endorphins at work rewarding the brain of the person who relinquishes some of their loose suggestibility. But it is such a pathetic problem of religion, as it does very little to meet the self-transcendence needs of the individual. Between the bursts of euphoria, the disorder causes people to feel guilty, depressed, and ashamed. Like other sufferers of monoideistic disturbances, they withdraw socially and retreat ever further into the cloistered world of their private religion. It is, without question, a syndrome contracted by "dead" Havers in a culture unable to pacify any longer its people with more effective self-transcending beliefs.

These are some of the reasons I feel that most of us are not ready to live with reality. No matter how foolish the means, we keep trying to escape, we never quit. Self-deception is again a *biological* urge. However, I have been saying throughout that we can no longer afford to live *outside* of reality. Our species cannot afford self-transcendence. So where does that leave us if we cannot live with illusion or without illusion? Is there, in fact, any hope for us as a species?

My reasoning tells me that we are on the road to self-extinction, that the cheerful robot is self-deceiving its way to disaster. I foresee us joining the dinosaurs and dodos because of our drive for reality-transcendence. We have seen a wide range of evidence to show that self-transcending belief, especially of the conventional variety, leads to the personality characteristics that stimulate people to become insensitive, intolerant, and cruel. Becker and Koestler show that all evil, including war, is largely the result of the self-transcendence that accompanies a rejection of reality. Self-transcendence enables us to abuse nature and destroy its harmony. If, in our self-transcendence, we do not kill ourselves directly, we may do it indirectly by continuing our present assault on the balance of nature. Also in that regard, we are standing on the threshold of self-extinction. We are showing few signs of *self-descending* sufficiently in order to see that we have almost totally destroyed our essential life-support systems.

Therefore, we see a powerful force in motion that could eventually see us exterminate ourselves since we cannot *come down to earth* and conquer our natural inclination toward self-deception and self-transcending beliefs. That possibility looms large given the strength of the paranormal belief imperative. Herzog asks, "Do you believe in transcendence downward?" I do not. Peter Berger, in *A Rumor of Angels*, said that *power* is the final illusion.[14] That I can believe. And that worries me even more. Although certain types of collective self-deception are in decline, others are taking their place. Collective ideologies appear and reappear in many forms. They will be the reason we use our suicidal weaponry on ourselves. The few meek voices that speak out in favor of an earth-bound view of ourselves are drowned by the crowd roaring that same deadly motto: "This is not the way it is!" We remain in the jaws of self-deception. We show no indication of outgrowing the paranormal belief imperative. The prospect is very slim that a true and non-destructive belief system will find its way into mass consciousness before we exterminate ourselves.

Einstein and Freud corresponded with each other regarding what, if anything, could be done to prevent the human race from destroying itself with its ever-more sophisticated weaponry. In one letter to Freud, Einstein expressed grave concern over "the disastrous collective suggestions that succeed so well in rousing men to such wild enthusiasm, even to sacrifice their lives." While referring to the "suicidal collective psychosis" that cultural suggestion can produce, Einstein asks Freud: "And so we come to our last question. Is it possible to control man's mental evolution so as to protect him against the psychoses of hate and destructiveness?"[15] That is exactly the question I have posed throughout this book. Einstein never saw a solution to the problem of our mental evolution. Until his death in 1955, he remained deeply worried that the human animal could not evolve out of its proneness to collective suggestion and the destructiveness associated with that characteristic. True to character, Freud held out very little hope in this regard. He replied to Einstein: "Why do we protest so vehemently against war, instead of just accepting it as another of life's importunities? For it seems a natural thing and practically unavoidable . . . *Communal,* not individual, violence will have its way."[16]

A primary reason I do not think we are capable of shedding our *communal* violence is because we are probably incapable of accepting the fact that we are alone. If we are to survive, Fromm writes in *Man for Himself* that man must:

acknowledge his fundamental aloneness and solitude in a universe indifferent to his fate, to recognize that there is no power transcending him which can solve his problem for him. Man must accept the responsibility for himself and the fact that only by using his own powers can he give meaning to his life. . . . If he faces the truth without panic he will recognize that *there is no meaning to life except the meaning man gives his life by the unfolding of his powers* . . . the one task that matters is the full development of our powers within the limitations of our existence.[17]

Therein lies the impossible solution. Our future hinges on the monumental task of collectively *not believing* in anything that transcends us, or in anything that allows us to transcend ourselves and each other. The impossible human challenge is to face the truth without panic, to derive all meaning from where we are and what we are. The gods would have to go. We would need to strip ourselves of all reality-transcending belief. But that is again too much to ask of a half-awake cultural zombie fixed cheerfully in the delusion that there is hope outside of ourselves.

Sartre also recognized that a truly *human* community would only be possible if we fully accepted the human condition *as it is.*

He believed that only then could we take *full* responsibility for each other and ourselves. This can be seen in his play *The Devil and the Good Lord*.[18] The play's hero, Goetz, realizes that God does not exist, and that God is really the *loneliness of man*. In his illumination, he deduces: "If God exists, man is nothing." Once God became an "absence," Goetz was overwhelmed by an awareness of how dependent we are on *each other*. He comments to his beloved, *"how real* you have become since He no longer exists," and then begs her never to turn her eyes from him lest he be terrorized by fear of annihilation. That is too idealistic. That exalted, but precarious, state is reserved for the few tormented and neurotic spirits who refuse the cultural sleep that weighs so heavily on our eyes. It is not for the masses.

For Sartre, life and people become *real* only when we become fully alone and condemned to freedom. Gods and all other transcendent beliefs make us and all of nature *unreal*. And, the more unreal we become, the less responsibility we take for each other, and the less compassion and empathy we feel for each other. We have already seen that it is easy and even satisfying to kill and hate what is not real. It is much more difficult to kill and hate what *is* real. The psychologist Rollo May once remarked that "one cannot love without death." To me, that says that the more removed we become from death and all other *realities* of our condition, the harder it is to love what is around us. But just as we reject reality, which often includes a denial of death, so we reject love. Although we see many expressions of it in our species, love is exceedingly difficult for us. Hate is much easier for an animal naturally hell-bent on deluding itself about its own existence. Killing is as close to truth as the human animal gets while transcended from itself.

We arrive again at the matter of hope. The real world would not offer enough *real* hope. We see in Dostoevsky's *The Idiot* someone who discovers that "God is a disease" but disregards that revelation because *it feels so good to believe*. He concludes that it would be worthwhile to give one's life for that "abnormal tension." That "tension" I have argued, has a biochemical basis. It is a *physical* tension that underlies the idiot in us. We are not ready to become miserable realists. The vast majority of us would rather believe that an escape-hatch exists in the form of Ishtar, one of the many good lords, the stars, or even mountains of money. For us, counter-intelligent belief is destined to remain preferable to intelligent unbelief.

I am glad to say that greater minds than my own disagree with me. Sartre, for example, believed we were capable of withstanding the despair that would stem from a reformulation of ourselves in our own image. In fact, in his play *The Flies*, he writes that "life *begins* on the far side of despair." Even Becker confessed to hope. Sam Keen had the privilege of interviewing Becker on his deathbed. In their discussion, some of Becker's statements suggest that hope could come from embracing what he so arduously argued was our greatest enemy – the truth. Becker remarked:

> Our critical task is the utter elimination of all consolations that are not empirically based. We need a *stark* picture of the human condition without false consolations . . . the courageous thing to do is look straight at the wintery smile on the face of truth.[19]

He went on to say that if we have a passion for the truth, we shall encounter a "temporary period of forlornness." He added that joy awaits us on the other side of this forlornness. He told Keen that "disillusionment must come before wisdom." Those words stood in such glaring contrast to his former disdain for hope. In fact, he had repeated Nikos Kazantzakis's sentiment that "hope is a rotten-thighed whore," who further distances us from a responsible acceptance of the human condition.

Becker's apparent volte-face on the subject of hope suddenly made sense when he disclosed that he too was a believer! He revealed himself as a believer in the same interview in which he spoke of the need to brace up against the wintery truth. The truth for Becker had changed with the birth of his first son. That, he said, was "the miracle that woke me up to the idea of God, seeing something pop in from the Void and seeing how magnificent it was, how much beyond our powers and our ken."[20] His dogged unbelief went out the window as he suddenly recognized that "this is God's world and everything is in His hands." The rotten-thighed whore had been transformed into the Almighty. Hope appeared everywhere with his "wakening to the divine," as he phrased it. Becker decided that, not only was it possible to face the truth of the human condition, but that it had meaning.

Had it not been for my state of shock, I would have cried at hearing the news of Becker's retreat into foolishness. Anyone but him! Especially amazing was the way that Becker had adhered to much of his earlier views about the essential worm-like nature of man, and the fundamentally evil nature of creation. He somehow juggled those views with his apparently opposing beliefs about the sublime works of the Creator. But I suppose one could say that there is no better way of showing that we are, in fact, contradictions and opposites. We were created in the image of a god as well as in the image of a worm. Why not believe both? Why not juggle opposites?

It is a strange type of coincidence that a similar thing happened to Rank earlier. After years as the great toppler of illusions, Rank stunned his followers by saying he had (like Kierkegaard) turned to religion. He explained himself to his intellectual supporters by saying that the most anyone can hope to do is *choose one's own form of foolishness*. Rank stuck to his view that no one, including himself, was intended to face reality alone. For Rank, it was a victory of sorts to be able to *choose* the type of "foolishness" that one will use to reinterpret reality. Rank regarded Christianity as a reasonably good system of foolishness and he made a conscious decision to incorporate a modified version of its beliefs.

What made Becker's surrender to religiosity different was his view that Christianity was flawed and dangerous. Becker stated:

> Christianity is in trouble not because its myths are dead, but because it does not offer its ideal of heroic sainthood as an immediate personal one to be *lived* by all believers . . . it has turned its back on the miraculousness of creation *and* the need to do something heroic *in this world* . . . the churches still bless unheroic wars and sanctify group hatred and victimage.[21]

For Becker, the message of love that Christ offered us had not sunk in. Becker viewed human love and charity as Pascal did – "feint and false images." Becker realized that Christian efforts to spread the words of love only fostered self-destruction. In that regard, I am reminded of the song, *Don't Look to Me*, by the talented Australian singer/songwriter Ross Ryan. There, Ryan reiterates the failure of Christianity to instill in people the virtues of love, tolerance, and peace. In the lyrics to that song, Jesus is repulsed and frustrated at the continuing ugliness of people. He decides to give up on humanity when he finally sees that people are more at home with hatred than love. Jesus realizes that he has been "sold out," that he has wasted his breath. Ryan's lyrics strike a somber but resonant chord as Jesus proclaims himself "the child who failed." He leaves us "on our crosses of plastic, with no one to answer our prayers."

All reality-rejecting beliefs are prayers for the healthy and pacifying "stupidity" of which Rank spoke. But even as a believer, Becker knew that some quests for stupidity were less deadly than others. For Becker, Christianity was not only that "failed child." As an *organized* attempt to spread the virtues that are sorely lacking in the human animal, Becker saw that it actually backfires and ends up "sanctifying" hatred. Despite his flight to the beyond, Becker never lost sight of the danger that looms as a result of *collective* illusion. Yet, like Einstein, Becker saw no solution, no clear way for a mass escape from the evil of collective suggestion.

Becker's "blindness" (if I dare use such a word to describe so great a thinker) was to take the form of a highly personal awe and respect for the supposed architect of creation. If that was the shape and extent of human self-deception, we might be safer than we are now from one another. But the fact remains that we are veritable pawns of culture and the victims of self-transcending beliefs. Furthermore, culture will continue to generate the nonsense we need and to pattern it into *collective* systems of counter-intelligence. I do not believe that reality-defying "foolishness" is a matter of choice. Still again, we are biologically incapable of choice in this matter. Beyond that, it would mean choosing despair and disillusionment over illusion. Our brains are programmed to be biased against reality. Our evolutionary design does not even allow most of us the dubious option of choosing clinical madness over absolute insanity. Given the option to kill each other in the image of the gods or to agonize *with* each other in the image of a worm, most will select the former. Nothing could be more in accord with our unworldly natures.

In his book *Beyond the Chains of Illusion*, Fromm professes a beleaguered optimism when he speaks of the perfectibility of the human being, while simultaneously doubting that sufficient time remains for us to rise above our suicidal impulses. Fromm expresses his personal fears about the future of our species, explaining his gloom as follows: "If we should all perish in the nuclear holocaust, it will not be because man was not capable of becoming human, or that he was inherently evil; it will be because the *consensus of stupidity* has prevented him from seeing reality and acting upon the truth."[22] It might be the case that the human being is not inherently evil in the strictest sense of the word, but evil and inhumanity seem to emerge with uncanny predictability. Throughout history, the human being has never been "human." Far more than coincidence is responsible for that fact. My fear is that the consensus of "stupidity" that now threatens our future is an inevitable product of our peculiar brain design. Furthermore, as Rank realized in his great moment of illumination, it is our greatest drive. Although we are not evil by the mere fact of birth, I believe that we are biologically burdened by this ancient evil-generating "stupidity" which protects as well as destroys our genius.

In a curious way, Canetti finds hope for our species. He admits that the one overriding question that remains is whether or not we can survive ourselves. In *Crowds and Power*, he aptly describes us as "rivals for the moon," a species that has stolen its own god and seized the god's weaponry of doom and terror. For Canetti, the suicidal element of our unusual evolutionary makeup is not extinct. The monster that lurks in us, he says, may eventually make Genghis Khan, Tamerlane, and Hitler seem like "pitiful amateurs." Despite all that, he sees hope in the fact that, more and more, we are becoming disciples and machines of the Industrial Age. Canetti regards production as incompatible with war. War is in decline, he says, because war costs people and therefore productive potential. Production wants people. As children of the god of Having, he thinks we could become programmed to the mentality of *"increase."* War and destruction mean *decrease.* Consequently, Canetti holds out hope that war might disappear of its own accord, that it will be perceived as too great an interruption to the actual process of production. For Canetti, the creatures of this new material spiritualism may be less destructive than the ones who have traditionally killed with so much determination and pleasure.

I leave open the possibility that there is substance to Canetti's optimism. And who am I to disregard completely the hope of Becker and Sartre that we could eventually surface more maturely on the far side of forlornness and despair? Still, I see nothing to suggest that we are about to be released from the tangle in which we find ourselves. For the foreseeable future, I believe that we shall remain cheerful prisoners aloft the wings of illusion. The truth is destined to remain what we feel it ought to be, not what it is. As we look out, layers of rose-colored glass prevent us from seeing that our wings have outworn their usefulness, that they have become devilishly entangled by our unique evolutionary heritage. There is unfortunately little that we can do to stop ourselves from crashing into the very weapon we used against our own intelligence. The nuclear age has transformed all forms of self-deception into a terrifying nemesis. Even so, all signs indicate that our wings will keep us too far removed from reality, and from each other, at a time when our feet must be firmly planted on the ground.

# Notes

## Preface

1 Wilder, T. (1967) *The Eighth Day*, New York: Harper & Row.
2 Carl Sagan used this phrase in his excellent documentary series, "Cosmos."
3 Rank described his own thought process in this manner. Cited in E. James Lieberman (1985) *Acts of Will: The Life and Work of Otto Rank*, New York: Free Press.

## Chapter 1 In search of ourselves

1 Rilke, R.M. (1977/1955) *Duino Elegies*, Boston: Houghton Mifflin.
2 Becker, E. (1973) *The Denial of Death*, New York: Free Press, p. 209.
3 Dewey, J. (1946) "The public and its problems: An essay in political inquiry." See Winn, R.B. (1959) *John Dewey: Dictionary of Education*, Westport, Conn.: Greenwood Press, p. 109.
4 Pirsig, R.M. (1974) *Zen and the Art of Motorcycle Maintenance*, London: Bodley Head.
5 I also postulated that built-in cognitive defenses may serve the purpose of safeguarding the self-deceptions that we use to invent alternative realities. See Schumaker, J.F. (1987) "Mental health, belief deficit compensation, and paranormal beliefs," *Journal of Psychology*, vol. 121, pp. 451-7.
6 This is an essential proposition of behavioral or learning theorists. Its roots are in the philosophical works of John Locke. For a more political perspective on this subject, see Castoriadis, C. (1967) *Modern Capitalism and Revolution*, London: Solidarity Press.
7 Cf. Rilke, *Duino Elegies*, p. 57.
8 Pascal, B. (1973/1960) *Pensées*, London: J.M. Dent, p. 65.

9 See Heider, K. (1976) "Dani sexuality: A low energy system," *MAN*, 11, 188–201.
10 Kennedy, E. (1977) *Believing*, Garden City, NY: Doubleday, p. 29.
11 Cf. Becker, *The Denial of Death*, p. 27.
12 Ibid., pp. 208–9.
13 Gould, S.J. (1977) *Ever since Darwin*, New York: W.W. Norton, p. 14.
14 See Clark, W. (1977) "Parapsychology and religion." in B. Wolman (ed.), *Philosophy and Parapsychology*, New York: Van Nostrand Reinhold. Also Le Shan, L. (1966) *The Medium, the Mystic, and the Physicist*, New York: Viking Press.
15 Cf. Gould, *Ever since Darwin*, p. 14.
16 See Bierce, A. (1946) *The Collected Writings of Ambrose Bierce*, New York: Citadel Press, p. 292.

## Chapter 2 The birth of the paranormal

1 Passingham, R.E. (1982) *The Human Primate*, Oxford: W.H. Freeman.
2 Schumaker, J.F., Barraclough, R.A., and Vagg, L.M. (1988) "Death anxiety in Malaysian and Australian university students," *Journal of Social Psychology*, vol. 128, pp. 41–7.
3 Bergson, H. (1935) *The Two Sources of Morality and Religion*, Westport, Conn.: Greenwood Press
4 Rieff, P. (1959) *Freud: The Mind of the Moralist*, Chicago: University of Chicago Press, p. 361.
5 Cf. Becker, E. (1973) *The Denial of Death*, New York: Free Press, p. 87.
6 Ibid., p. 26.
7 Ibid., p. 263.
8 Crook, J. (1980) *The Evolution of Human Consciousness*, Oxford: Clarendon Press, p. 353.
9 Dobzhansky, T., Ayala, F.J., Stebbins, G.L., and Valentine, J.W. (1977) *Evolution*, San Francisco: W.H. Freeman, p. 454.
10 Konner, M. (1982) *The Tangled Wing: Biological Constraints on the Human Spirit*, New York: Harper & Row, p. 354.
11 Zilboorg, G. (1943) "Fear of death," *Psychoanalytic Quarterly*, vol. 12, pp. 465–75, 467.
12 James, W. (1902/1958) *Varieties of Religious Experience: A Study in Human Nature*, New York: Mentor Edition, p. 281.
13 Berger, P.L. (1967) *The Sacred Canopy: Elements of a Sociological Theory of Religion*, Garden City, NJ: Doubleday.
14 Ortega y Gasset, J. (1957) *The Revolt of the Masses*, New York: W. W. Norton, pp. 156–7.
15 Berger, P.L. (1969) *A Rumour of Angels*, Harmondsworth: Penguin Books, p. 95.
16 Case, C. C. (1977) *Culture, The Human Plan: Essays in the Anthropo-*

*logical Interpretation of Human Behavior*, Washington, DC: University Press of America, p. 44.
17 Ibid., p. 41.
18 Cf. Becker, *The Denial of Death*, p. 283.
19 Cf. Wilder, T. (1967) *The Eighth Day*, New York: Harper & Row, p. 134.
20 For an overview of Wheeler's ideas, see Gliedman, J. (1984) "Turning Einstein upside down," *Science Digest*, October.
21 Ross's ideas regarding randomness are mentioned in Cornell, J. (1984) "Science versus the paranormal," *Psychology Today*, March.
22 La Barre, W. (1972) *The Ghost Dance: Origins of Religion*, London: Allen & Unwin, p. 12.
23 Feibleman, J.R. (1963) *Mankind Behaving*. Springfield, Ill.: C. C. Thomas.
24 Cf. Bergson, *Two Sources of Morality and Religion*, p. 194.
25 Ibid., p. 99.
26 Ibid., p. 99.
27 Ibid., pp. 92–4.
28 Spiro, M.E. (1965) "Culturally constituted defense mechanisms," in M. E. Spiro (ed.), *Context and Meaning in Cultural Anthropology*, New York: Free Press.
29 Ibid., p. 100.
30 Cf. Pascal, B. (1973/1960) *Pensées*, London: J.M. Dent, p. 40.
31 Kierkegaard, S. (1849/1954) *The Sickness unto Death*, New York: Anchor Edition.
32 Cf. Becker, *The Denial of Death*, p. 55.
33 Freud, S. (1930/1969) *Civilization and its Discontents*, London: Hogarth Press, p. 81.
34 Hoffer, E. (1951) *The True Believer*, New York: Harper & Row, p. 75.
35 Freud, S. (1933/1973) *New Introductory Lectures on Psychoanalysis*, Harmondsworth: Penguin Books.

## Chapter 3 Suggestibility and waking hypnosis

1 Rank, O. (1936/1945) *Will Therapy, Truth and Reality*, New York: Knopf, pp. 251–2.
2 Russell, B. (1916) *Principles of Social Reconstruction*, cited in Fromm, E. (1981) *On Disobedience and Other Essays*, New York: Seabury Press, pp. 49–50.
3 Cf. Konner, M.(1982) *The Tangled Wing: Biological Constraints on the Human Spirit*, New York: Harper & Row, p. 327.
4 Haraldsson, E. (1985) "Interrogative suggestibility and its relationship with personality, perceptual defensiveness and extraordinary beliefs," *Personality and Individual Differences*, vol. 6, pp. 765–7.
5 Chertok, L. (1984) "On the centenary of Charcot: hysteria, suggest-

ibility and hypnosis," *British Journal of Medical Psychology*, vol. 57, pp. 111–20.

6 Kihlstrom, J.F. (1985) "Hypnosis," *Annual Review of Psychology*, vol. 36, pp. 385–418.

7 Orne, M. (1959) "The nature of hypnosis," *Journal of Abnormal and Social Psychology*, vol. 58, pp. 277–99.

8 Rossi, E.L. (1986) "Altered states of consciousness in everyday life," in B. Wolman and M. Ullman (eds), *Handbook of States of Consciousness*. New York: Van Nostrand Reinhold, p. 97.

9 Fromm, E. (1981) *On Disobedience and Other Essays*, New York: Seabury Press, p. 43.

10 Ferenczi, S. (1916/1952) *First Contributions to Psycho-Analysis*, translated by E. Jones, London: The Hogarth Press, pp. 84–5.

11 McDougall, W. (1926/1960) "Outline of abnormal psychology," in M. Brenman and M. Gill (eds), *Hypnotherapy*, New York: International Universities Press, p. 101.

12 Freud, S. (1921/1965) *Group Psychology and the Analysis of Ego*, New York: Bantam Books, p. 60.

13 Fenichel, O. (1944) "Psychoanalytic remarks on Fromm's book 'Escape from Freedom'," *Psychoanalytic Review*, vol. 31, pp. 133–4.

14 See Alcock, J.E. (1981) *Parapsychology, Science or Magic: A Psychological Perspective*, Oxford: Pergamon Press, pp. 16–20.

15 Vetter, G.B. (1973) *Magic and Religion*, New York: Philosophical Library, p. 227.

16 Henslin, J.M. (1967) "Craps and magic," *American Journal of Sociology*, vol. 73, pp. 316–30.

17 Cf. Vetter, *Magic and Religion*; also Jahoda, G. (1969) *The Psychology of Superstition*, Harmondsworth: Penguin Books.

18 Solomon, R.L. (1982) "The opponent process in acquired motivation," in D. Pfaff (ed.), *The Physiological Mechanisms of Motivation*, New York: Springer-Verlag, pp. 321–2.

19 Olds, J. and Milner, P. (1954) "Positive reinforcement produced by electrical stimulation of septal area and other regions of the rat brain," *Journal of Comparative and Physiological Psychology*, vol. 47, pp. 419–27.

20 Halperin, R. and Pfaff, D.W. (1982) "Brain-stimulated reward and control of autonomic function: Are they related?" in D. Pfaff (ed.), *The Physiological Mechanisms of Motivation*, New York: Springer-Verlag, pp. 337–73.

21 Knox, V.J., Morgan, A.H. and Hilgard, E.R. (1974) "Pain and suffering in ischemia: The paradox of hypnotically suggested anesthesia as contradicted by reports from the hidden observer," *Archives of General Psychiatry*, vol. 30, pp. 840–7.

22 Hilgard, J.R. and LeBaron, S. (1982) "Relief of anxiety and pain in children and adolescents with cancer," *International Journal of Clinical Hypnosis*, vol. 30, pp. 417–42; also, Hilgard, J.R. and LeBaron, S.

(1984) *Hypnosis in the Treatment of Pain and Anxiety in children with cancer*, Los Altos, Calif.: Kaufmann.
23 See Levine, J.D., Gordon, N.C., and Fields, H.L. (1978) "The mechanism of placebo analgesia," *Lancet*, vol. 2, pp. 654–7.
24 See Sackeim, H. A. and Gur, R.C. (1978) "Self-deception, self-confrontation, and consciousness," in G. Schwartz and D. Shapiro (eds), *Consciousness and Self-Regulation: Advances in Theory and Research*, New York: Plenum Press, pp. 188–9.
25 Ibid., p. 149.
26 Orne, M.T. (1959) "The nature of hypnosis: Artifact and essence,"*Journal of Abnormal and Social Psychology*, vol. 58, pp. 277–99.
27 Hilgard, E.R. (1977) *Divided Consciousness: Multiple Controls in Human Thought and Action*, New York: John Wiley.
28 Fingarette, H. (1969) *Self-Deception*, London: Routledge & Kegan Paul.
29 Sperry, R.W. (1968) "Hemispheric deconnection and unity in conscious awareness," *American Psychologist*, vol. 23, pp. 723–33.
30 Ornstein, R.E. (1972) *The Psychology of Consciousness*, San Francisco: W. H. Freeman.
31 Cf. Sackeim and Gur, *Consciousness and Self-Regulation: Advances in Theory*, p. 188.
32 See Gur, R.C. and Gur, R.E. (1974) "Handedness, sex and eyedness as moderating variables in the relation between hypnotic susceptibility and functional brain asymmetry," *Journal of Abnormal Psychology*, vol. 83, pp. 635–43; also Gur, R.E. and Reyher, J. (1973) "The relationship between style of hypnotic induction and lateral eye movement," *Journal of Abnormal Psychology*, vol. 82, pp. 499–505; also Bakan, P. (1969) "Hypnotizability, laterality of eye movement and functional symmetry," *Perceptual and Motor Skills*, vol. 28, pp. 927–32.

## Chapter 4 Culture: the master hypnotist

1 Rohner, R.P. (1984) "Toward a conception of culture for cross-cultural psychology," *Journal of Cross-Cultural Psychology*, vol. 15, pp. 111–38.
2 Ibid., p. 112.
3 Rossides, R.P. (1968) *Society as a Functional Process*, Toronto: McGraw-Hill, p. 87.
4 Cf. Rohner, "Toward a conception of culture," pp. 119–20.
5 Dawson is cited in Keesing, R.M. (1974) "Theories of culture," *Annual Review of Anthropology*, vol. 3, pp. 73–97.
6 Reynolds, V. and Tanner, R.E. (1983) *The Biology of Religion*, London: Longman.
7 See Cawte, J. (1966) "The meaning of subincision of the urethra to

Aboriginal Australians," *British Journal of Medical Psychology*, vol. 39, 245-53.

8 Cf. Becker, E. (1973) *The Denial of Death*, New York: Free Press, pp. 198–9.

9 Ibid., p. 188.

10 Cf. Wilder, T. (1967) *The Eighth Day*, New York: Harper & Row, p. 18.

11 Cf. La Barre, W. (1972) *The Ghost Dance: Origins of Religion*, London: Allen & Unwin, p. 1.

12 Shaffer, P. (1974) *Equus*, New York: Avon Books.

13 Shames, M.L. (1981) "Hypnotic susceptibility and conformity: On the mediational mechanism of suggestibility," *Psychological Reports*, vol. 49, pp. 563–6.

14 Rank, O. (1936/1945) *Will Therapy, Truth and Reality*, New York: Knopf, p. 195; cited in Becker, *The Denial of Death*, p. 178.

15 Schilder, P. (1959) in M. Gill and M. Brenman (eds), *Hypnosis and Related States*, New York: Science Editions, p. 159.

16 Cf. Case, C.C. (1977) *Culture, The Human Plan: Essays in the Anthropological Interpretation of Human Behavior*, Washington, DC: University Press of America, p. 44.

17 Ibid., p. 13.

18 Cf. Berger, P.L. (1967) *The Sacred Canopy: Elements of a Sociological Theory of Religion*, Garden City, NJ: Doubleday, p. 27.

19 Cf. Hoffer, E. (1951) *The True Believer*, New York: Harper & Row, p. 76.

20 Osherow, N. (1984) "Making sense of the nonsensical: An analysis of Jonestown," in E. Aronson (ed.), *The Social Animal*, New York: W. H. Freeman.

21 See Naroll, R. (1983) *The Moral Order*, London: Sage, p. 375.

22 Fromm, E. (1956) *The Sane Society*, London: Kegan Paul, p. 16.

23 Riesman, D. (1973) *The Lonely Crowd: A Study of the Changing American Character*, New York: Yale University Press, p. 83.

## Chapter 5 Paranormal belief: our cruel savior

1 Worsley, P. (1970) *The Trumpet Shall Sound*, London: Paladin.

2 McClure, R.F. and Loden, M. (1982) "Religious activity, denomination memberships and life satisfaction," *Psychology*, vol. 19, pp. 12–17; also see McClain, E.W. (1978) "Personality differences between intrinsically religious and nonreligious students – factor analytic study," *Journal of Personality Assessment*, vol. 42, pp. 159–66; also Ness, R.C. and Wintrob, R.M. (1980) "The emotional impact of fundamentalistic religious participation," *American Journal of Orthopsychiatry*, vol. 50, pp. 202–15; also Sturgeon, R.S. and Hamley, R.W.

(1971) "Religiosity and anxiety," *Journal of Social Psychology*, vol. 108, pp. 137–8.

3 Hay, D. and Morisy, M. (1978) "Reports of ecstatic, paranormal or religious experience in Great Britain and the United States," *Journal for the Scientific Study of Religion*, vol. 17, pp. 238–55.

4 Maris, R.W. (1981) *Pathways to Suicide*, Baltimore, MD: Johns Hopkins University Press; also Martin, R.W. (1984) "Religiosity and United States suicide rates," *Journal of Clinical Psychology*, vol. 40, pp. 1166–9.

5 Camus, A. (1955) *The Myth of Sisyphus*, London: Hamish Hamilton.

6 Freud, S. (1964/1927) *The Future of an Illusion*, New York: Anchor Books, p. 77.

7 Schumaker, J.F. (1987) "Mental health, belief deficit compensation, and paranormal beliefs," *Journal of Psychology*, vol. 121, pp. 451–7.

8 For the Paranormal Belief Scale, see Tobacyck, J. and Milford, G. (1983) "Belief in paranormal phenomena: Assessment instrument development and implications for personality functioning," *Journal of Personality and Social Psychology*, vol. 44, pp. 1029–37.

9 See Bainbridge, W.S. (1981) "Biorhythms: Evaluating a pseudoscience," in K. Frazier (ed.), *Paranormal Borderlands of Science*, Buffalo, NY: Prometheus; also Randall, T.M. and Desrosiers, M. (1980) "Measurements of supernatural beliefs," *Journal of Personality Assessment*, vol. 44, 493–8; also Alcock, *Parapsychology: Science or Magic*, pp. 28–30.

10 For a brief summary of the research on this subject, see Argyle, M. (1973) "Seven psychological roots of religion," in L.B. Brown (ed.), *Psychology and Religion*, Harmondsworth: Penguin Books, p. 25.

11 Spellman, C.M., Baskett, G.D. and Byrne, D. (1971) "Manifest anxiety as a contributing factor in religious conversion," *Journal of Consulting and Clinical Psychology*, vol. 36, pp. 245–7.

12 Cf. Tobacyk and Milford, *Journal of Personality and Social Psychology*; also Jeffers, F.C., Nichols, C.R. and Eisdorfer, C. (1961) "Attitudes of older persons to death," *Journal of Gerontology*, vol. 16, pp. 53–6.

13 See D.O. Moberg (1973) "Religiosity in old age," in L.B. Brown (ed.), *Psychology and Religion*, Harmondsworth: Penguin Books, p. 204.

14 Kubler-Ross, E. (1975) *Death: The Final Stage of Growth*, Englewood Cliffs, NJ: Prentice-Hall.

15 Westman, A.S. and Canter, F.M. (1985) "Fear of death and the concept of extended self," *Psychological Reports*, vol. 56, pp. 419–25.

16 Cf. Schumaker, J. et al. (1988) "Death anxiety in Malaysian and Australian university students," *Journal of Social Psychology*, vol. 128, pp. 41–7.

17 Blum, S.H. and Blum. L.H. (1974) "Do's and don'ts: An informal study of some prevailing superstitions," *Psychological Reports*, vol. 35, pp. 567–71.

18 See Jahoda, G. (1969) *The Psychology of Superstition*, Harmondsworth: Penguin Books.

19 Tobacyk, J. (1984) "Death threat, death concerns, and paranormal belief," in F. Epting and R. Neimeyer (eds), *Personal Meanings of Death*, New York: McGraw-Hill.
20 See Jones, W., Russell, D. and Nickel, T. (1977) "Belief in the paranormal scale: an objective instrument to measure belief in magical phenomena and causes," *JSAS Catalog of Selected Documents in Psychology*, vol. 7, pp. 100 (ms. No. 1577).
21 Rokeach, M. (1960) *The Open and Closed Mind*, New York: Basic Books.
22 Martin, D.J., Abramson, L.Y. and Alloy, L.B. (1984) "Illusion of control for self and others in depressed and nondepressed college students," *Journal of Personality and Social Psychology*, vol. 46, pp. 125–36.
23 Batson, C.D. and Ventis, W.L. (1982) *The Religious Experience: A Social-Psychological Perspective*, Oxford: Oxford University Press.
24 "To deny our nothingness" is the marvelous title of Maurice Friedman's book (1984), Chicago: University of Chicago Press.
25 Cf. Rilke, R.M. *Duino Elegies*, Boston: Houghton Mifflin.
26 Cf. Becker, E. (1973) *The Denial of Death*, New York: Free Press, p. 244.
27 See *The Journal of the Otto Rank Association*, June 1967, p. 118.
28 Crandall, V.C. and Gozali, J. (1969) "Social desirability responses of children of four religious-cultural groups," *Child Development*, vol. 40, pp. 751–62.
29 Pohier, J.M. (1965) "Religious mentality and infantile mentality," in A. Godin (ed.), *Child and Adult before God*, Chicago: Loyola University Press, pp. 19–42.
30 Alcock, J.E. and Otis, L.P. (1980) "Critical thinking and belief in the paranormal," *Psychological Reports*, vol. 46, pp. 479–82.
31 Alcock, J. (1981) *Parapsychology: Science or Magic*, New York: Pergamon Press, p. 53.
32 Brown, L.B. (1973) "A study of religious belief," in L.B. Brown (ed.), *Psychology and Religion*, Harmondsworth: Penguin Books, p. 48.
33 See Prothero, E.T. and Jensen, J.A. (1950) "Interrelations of religious and ethnic attitudes in selected southern populations," *Journal of Social Psychology*, vol. 32, pp. 45–9; also Wilson, W.C. (1960) "Extrinsic religious values and prejudice," *Journal of Abnormal Social Psychology*, vol. 60, pp. 286–8; also Argyle, M. (1958) *Religious Behavior*, London: Routledge & Kegan Paul.
34 Ellis, A. (1975) "The case against religion: A psychotherapist's view," in B. Ard (ed.), *Counseling and Psychotherapy: Classics on Theories and Issues*, Palo Alto, Calif.: Science and Behavior Books, p. 440.
35 Cf. Argyle, *Religious Behavior*, p. 84.
36 Allport, G.W. and Ross, J.M. (1967) "Personal religious orientation and prejudice," *Journal of Personality and Social Psychology*, vol. 51, pp. 432–43.
37 Byrnes, J.F. (1984) *The Psychology of Religion*, New York: Free Press, p. 199.
38 Batson, C.D., Schoenrade, P.A. and Pych, V. (1985) "Brotherly love or

self-concern?: Behavioral consequences of religion," in L.B. Brown (ed.), *Advances in the Psychology of Religion*, New York: Pergamon Press.
39 Ibid., p. 189.
40 Kirkpatrick, C. (1949) "Religion and humanitarianism: A study of institutional implications," *Psychological Monographs*, vol. 63, no. 304.
41 Allport, G.W. and Kramer, B.M. (1946) "Some roots of prejudice," *Journal of Psychology*, vol. 22, pp. 9–30.
42 Stouffer, S.A. (1955) *Communism, Conformity, and Civil Liberties*, New York: Doubleday.
43 Hong, J. (1984) "Australian attitudes towards homosexuality," *Journal of Psychology*, vol. 117, pp. 89–95.
44 Adorno, T., Frenkel-Brunswicke, E., Levinson, D., and Sanford, N. (1950) *The Authoritarian Personality*, New York: Harper.
45 Dixon's research was presented at the 1988 conference of the New Zealand Psychological Society. A summary of this study appeared in Christchurch's principal newspaper, *The Press*, on 19 August 1988.
46 Cited in Cornell, J. (1984) "Science versus the paranormal," *Psychology Today*, March, pp. 28–33.
47 McClaren, E. (1976) *The Nature of Belief*, New York: Hawthorne Books, p. 57.
48 Sir Hermann Bondi's essay appears in *Lying Truths*, an edited work by R. Duncan and M. Weston-Smith (1979), Oxford: Pergamon Press, pp. 204–10.
49 Duncan, H.D. (1962) *Communication and Social Order*, New York: Bedminster Press, p. 131.
50 George, H. (1934/1981) *Social Problems*, New York: Robert Schalkenbach Foundation, p. 31.
51 Cf. Becker, E. (1973) *The Denial of Death*, New York: Free Press, p. 145.
52 Ibid., p. 149.
53 Becker, E. (1975) *Escape from Evil*, New York: Free Press, p. 96.
54 Ibid., p. 96.
55 Ibid., p. 50.
56 Ibid., p. 162.
57 Reich, W. (1933/1970) *The Mass Psychology of Fascism*, New York: Farrar-Straus, p. 334.
58 Cf. Becker, *The Denial of Death*, p. 227.
59 Koestler, A. (1967) *The Ghost in the Machine*, London: Hutchinson, p. 240.
60 Ibid., p. 218.
61 Ibid., p. 251.
62 Ibid., pp. 250–1.
63 Cf. Becker, *Escape from Evil*, p. 169.
64 Ibid., p. 139.
65 Ibid., p. 134.
66 Ibid., p. 141.

67 Ibid., p. 116.
68 Duncan, H.D. (1962) *Communication and Social Disorder*, New York: Bedminster Press, p. 127; cited in Becker, *Escape from Evil*, p. 116.
69 Fromm, E. (1964) *The Heart of Man: Its Genius for Good and Evil*, New York: Harper & Row.
70 Cf. Becker, *Escape from Evil*, p. 147.
71 See Zimbardo, P.G. (1970) "The human choice: Individuation, reason, and order versus deindividuation, impulse, and chaos," in W. Arnold and D. Levine (eds), *Nebraska Symposium on Motivation*, vol. 17, Lincoln, Neb.: University of Nebraska Press.
72 Prentice-Dunn, S. and Rogers, R.W. (1982) "Effects of public and private self-awareness on deindividuation and aggression," *Journal of Personality and Social Psychology*, vol. 43, pp. 503–13; also see Fenigstein, A., Scheier, M.F. and Buss, A.M. (1975) "Public and private self-consciousness: assessment and theory," *Journal of Consulting and Clinical Psychology*, vol. 43, pp. 522–7.
73 Scheier, M.F., Carver, C.S., and Gibbons, F.X. (1979) "Self-directed attention, awareness of bodily states and suggestibility," *Journal of Personality and Social Psychology*, vol. 37, pp. 1576–88.

## Chapter 6 The clumsy lie

1 Cf. Becker, E. (1973) *The Denial of Death*, New York: Free Press, p. 201.
2 Ibid., p. 178.
3 Heirich, H. (1977) "Change of heart: A test of some widely held theories about religious conversion," *American Journal of Sociology*, vol. 83, pp. 653–79.
4 See Bruch, H. (1973) *Eating Disorders*, New York: Basic Books; also *The Golden Cage* (1978), Cambridge, Mass.: Harvard University Press.
5 Cf. Koestler, A. (1967) *The Ghost in the Machine*, London: Hutchinson, p. 177.
6 See Bruch, H. (1975) "How to treat anorexia nervosa," *Roche Reports: Frontiers of Psychiatry*, pp. 1–2; also Selvini, M. (1971) "Anorexia nervosa," in S. Arieti (ed.), *World Biennial of Psychiatry and Psychotherapy*, vol. 1, New York: Basic Books.
7 Kaffman, M. (1981) "Monoideism in psychiatry: theoretical and clinical implications," *American Journal of Psychotherapy*, vol. 35, pp. 235–43.
8 Kaffman, M. (1984) "Inflexible belief constructs in families of paranoid patients," *International Journal of Family Psychiatry*, vol. 3, pp. 487–500.
9 "Trance logic" refers to the illogic observed in hypnotic subjects. See Orne, M. (1972) "On the simulating subject as a quasi-control group in hypnotic research," in E. Fromm and R.E. Shor (eds), *Hypnosis: Research, Developments, and Perspectives*, Chicago: Aldine.

10  Garner, D.M. and Garfinkel, P.E. (1979) "The Eating Attitude Test: An index of the symptoms of anorexia nervosa," *Psychological Medicine*, vol. 9, pp. 1–7.

11  Groth-Marnat, G. and Schumaker, J.F. (in press) "Hypnotizability, attitude toward eating, and concern for body size in female college students," *American Journal of Clinical Hypnosis*.

12  Long, T.E. (1968) "Some early-life stimulus correlates of hypnotizability," *The International Journal of Clinical and Experimental Hypnosis*, vol. 16, pp. 61–7.

13  Cf. Crook, J. (1980) *The Evolution of Human Consciousness*, Oxford: Clarendon Press, p. 306.

14  Kierkegaard, S. (1849/1954) *Sickness Unto Death*, translated by Walter Lowrie, New York: Anchor Books, pp. 174–5.

15  See Bruch, H. (1974) *Eating Disorders*, London: Routledge & Kegan Paul; also Buhrich, N. (1981) "Frequency of presentation of anorexia nervosa in Malaysia," *Australian and New Zealand Journal of Psychiatry*, vol. 15, pp. 153–5.

16  For a brief overview of koro, see Rin, H. (1965) "A study of the aetiology of koro in respect to the Chinese concept of illness," *International Journal of Psychiatry*, vol. 11, pp. 7–13; also Yap, P.M. (1965) "Koro – a culture-bound depersonalization syndrome," *British Journal of Psychiatry*, vol. 111, pp. 43–50.

17  Temoshok, L. and Attkisson, C.C. (1977) "Epidemiology of hysterical phenomena: Evidence for a psychosocial theory," in M. Horowitz (ed.), *Hysterical Personality*, New York: Jason Aronson, p. 207.

18  Ibid., p. 206; see also Wittkower, E.D. and Dubreuil, G. (1968) "Cultural factors in mental illness," in N. Norbeck (ed.), *The Study of Personality*, New York: Holt, Rinehart & Winston.

19  See Edwards, J.W. (1983) "Semen anxiety in South Asian cultures: Cultural and transcultural significance," *Medical Anthropology*, Summer, pp. 51–76; also Langness, L.L. (1967) "Hysterical psychosis – the cross-cultural evidence," *American Journal of Psychiatry*, vol. 124, pp. 143–51; and Murphy, H.B. (1973) "History and evolution of syndromes: the striking case of latah and amok," in M. Hammer, K. Salzinger and S. Sutton (eds), *Psychopathology*, New York: John Wiley.

20  Cf. Kaffman, "Inflexible belief constructs in families of paranoid patients," p. 497.

21  Ibid., p. 497.

22  Ibid., p. 492.

23  Ibid., p. 493.

24  Trainor, D. (1981) "Analgesia seen in altered states of consciousness," *Psychiatric News*, vol. 16, pp. 19–24.

25  Cf. Kaffman, "Inflexible belief constructs," p. 487; also see Kaffman M. (1981) "Paranoid disorders: The core of truth behind the

delusional system," *International Journal of Family Therapy*, vol. 3, pp. 21–30.

26 Ibid., p. 488.
27 Ibid., p. 497.
28 Ibid., p. 492.
29 Bliss, E.L. (1983) "Multiple personalities, related disorders, and hypnosis," *American Journal of Clinical Hypnosis*, vol. 26, pp. 114–23.
30 See Andorfer, J.C. (1985) "Multiple personality in the human information processor," *Journal of Clinical Psychology*, vol. 41, pp. 309–24; also Gillet, G.R. (1986) "Multiple personality and the concept of a person," *New Ideas in Psychology*, vol. 2, pp. 173–84.
31 Spiegel, D. (1984) "Multiple personality as a post-traumatic disorder," *Psychiatric Clinics of North America*, vol. 7, pp. 101–10.
32 Kennedy, J.G. (1977) "Nubian Zar ceremonies as psychotherapy," in D. Lawdy (ed.), *Culture, Disease and Healing: Studies in Medical Anthropology*, New York: Macmillan, pp. 375–84.
33 See Ward, C. (1984) "Thaipusam in Malaysia," *Ethos*, vol. 12, pp. 307–34. Colleen Ward is now at Canterbury University in New Zealand.
34 See Lex, B. (1975) "Physiological aspects of ritual trance," *Journal of Altered States of Consciousness*, vol. 2, pp. 109–22.
35 Kiev, A. (1964) *Magic, Faith and Healing: Studies in Primitive Psychiatry Today*, New York: Free Press.
36 Huxley, A. (1961) *The Devils of London*, London: Chatto & Windus, p. 369.
37 Jilek, W.G. (1972) "'Brainwashing' as therapeutic technique in contemporary Canadian Indian spirit dancing," in J. Westermeyer (ed.), *Anthropology and Mental Health*, The Hague, Netherlands: Mouton Press.
38 Varma, V.K. (1988) "Culture, personality and psychotherapy," *The International Journal of Social Psychiatry*, vol. 34, pp. 142–9.
39 Richardson, J.T. (1984) "Conversion, brainwashing, and deprogramming," in M. Walraven and H. Fitzgerald (eds), *Annual Editions in Psychology*, 84/85, Guildford, Conn.: Dushkin.
40 Hafeiz, H.B. (1980) "Hysterical conversion: A prognostic study," *British Journal of Psychiatry*, vol. 136, pp. 548–51.
41 Rank, O. (1958/1941) *Beyond Psychology*, New York: Dover Books, p. 49.
42 Cf. Becker, E. (1973) *The Denial of Death*, New York: Free Press, p. 191.
43 See Engstrom, D.R. (1976) "Hypnotic susceptibility, EEG-Alpha, and self-regulation," in G. Schwartz and D. Shapiro (eds), *Consciousness and Self-Regulation*, New York: Plenum.
44 Gorassini, D.R. and Spanos, N.P. (1986) "A social-cognitive skills approach to the successful modification of hypnotic susceptibility," *Journal of Personality and Social Psychology*, vol. 50, pp. 1004–12; see also Spanos, N.P., de Groh, M. and de Groot, H. (1987) "Skill training

for enhancing hypnotic susceptibility and word list amnesia," *British Journal of Experimental and Clinical Hypnosis*, vol. 4, pp. 15–23.

## Chapter 7 The unthinkable edge

1 Beckett, S. (1958) *Endgame: A play in one Act*, translated by the author, New York: Grove Press.
2 See Gelwick, R. (1979) "Post-critical belief," in R. Fitzgerald (ed.), *The Sources of Hope*, Oxford: Pergamon Press, p. 132.
3 Cf. Kierkegaard, S. (1849/1954) *The Sickness Unto Death*, New York: Anchor Edition, p. 181.
4 Cf. Bellow, S. (1964) *Herzog*, Harmondsworth: Penguin Books, p. 317.
5 Cain, M.S. (1983) "Psychic surrender: America's creeping paralysis," *The Humanist*, vol. 32, pp. 5–11.
6 Ibid., p. 224.
7 Ibid.
8 Cf. Becker, E. (1975) *Escape from Evil*, New York: Free Press, p. 156.
9 Canetti, E. (1960) *Crowds and Power*, Harmondsworth: Penguin Books, p. 543.
10 Cf. Becker, *Escape from Evil*, p. 165.
11 Fromm, E. (1981) "Values, psychology, and human existence," in E. Fromm, *On Disobedience and Other Essays*, New York: Seabury Press, p. 15.
12 Ibid., p. 15.
13 Ibid., p. 13.
14 Cf. Berger, P. L. (1969) *A Rumour of Angels*, Harmondsworth: Penguin Books, p. 91.
15 Einstein wrote this letter to Freud in July 1932.
16 Freud's reply to Einstein was written in September 1932.
17 Fromm, E. (1947) *Man for Himself: An Inquiry into the Psychology of Ethics*, New York: Rinehart, p. 45 (italics in original).
18 Sartre, J.P. (1960) *The Devil and the Good Lord*, New York: Knopf.
19 See Keen, S. (1974) "The heroics of everyday life: A theorist of death confronts his own end," *Psychology Today*, April, pp. 71–80.
20 Ibid., p. 79.
21 Cf. Becker, *Escape from Evil*, p. 164.
22 Fromm, E. (1962) *Beyond the Chains of Illusion*, New York: Simon and Schuster, p. 182 (my emphasis).

# Index

Orne, Martin
  on features of hypnosis, 43
  on trance logic, 56
Ornstein, Robert, 58
Orsherow, Neal, on Jonestown
    massacre, 74
Ortega y Gasset, José, on chaos of
    life, 23

paranoia, 10, 130–3
  as autosuggestive disorder, 130
  family patterns in, 131
paranormal belief imperative, 5
Pascal, Blaise, 3, 30, 35, 73, 103, 161
Passingham, R. E., on
    consciousness, 17
penis, subincision of, 69
phobias, 133
Pirsig, Robert, 2
Pohier, Jacques, 93
prejudice, and religiosity, 96–7
Prentice-Dunn, Steven and
    Rogers, Ronald, on aggression
    and self-awareness, 105–6
psychoanalysis, inadequacy of, 36
psychology
  inadequacy of, 1
  self-consciousness of, 9
psychotherapy, 134–47
  and brain hemisphericity, 136
  non-Western methods of, 135–
    41, 144
  and symptom substitution, 144

Rank, Otto, 8, 11, 21, 31, 71, 152
  on despair of Westerners, 76
  on "legitimate foolishness," 145
  on need for illusion, 39, 68
reality
  and chaos, 25–6
  danger of seeing, 20
  definition of, 8
  distortion of, 5
  need to escape, 30–5
  senseless nature of, 19
  as "too real," 23

Reich, Wilhelm, 100–1
religion
  belief in, 75
  biology of, 66–8
  and culture, 77
  as evolutionary strategy, 12
  modern, as business, 154
  problems with Roman Catholic,
    88
  and psychotherapy, 144
Reynolds, Vernon and Tanner,
    Ralph, on biology of religion,
    66–7
Richardson, James, on
    deprogramming, 142
Riesman, David, 77
Rilke, Rainer Maria, 1, 3, 27, 90
Rohner, Ronald, on definition of
    culture, 63–4
Rokeach, Milton, on Roman
    Catholic religion, 88
Ross, Lee, on problem of
    randomness, 25
Rossi, Ernest, on "common
    everyday trance," 44
Rossides, R. P., on cultural control,
    64
Russell, Bertrand, on fear of
    thinking, 39–40
Ryan, Ross, on failure of
    Christianity, 161

Sackeim, Harold and Gur, Ruben
  on biology of self-deception,
    55–60
  on criteria for self-deception, 55
Sartre, Jean Paul, 90, 149, 158–60
Schaffer, Peter, on "normality,"
    70–1
Scheier, Michael, on suggestibility
    and self-awareness, 106–7
Schilder, Paul, 71
Schweitzer, Albert, on Western
    people, 76
self-awareness
  loss of, 92–4

pros and cons of, 18
self-deception, 5, 151
  and depression, 89
  physiology of, 57–9
self-transcendence
  dangers of, 100–5
  paradox of, 103
sexual drive, 6–7
Shames, Morris, on conformity
  and suggestibility, 71
Solomon, Richard, on motivational
  systems, 51
Sperry, R. W., on "split-brain," 58
Spiegel, David, on multiple
  personality disorder, 133
Spiro, Melford, 35, 129
  on "absolute insanity," 29–30
  on religious drive, 12
Streiker, Lowell, 97
stupidity, as powerful drive, 39
suggestibility, 38–61
  in anorexia nervosa, 112–17
  and endorphins, 46
  enhancement of, 146
  and hypnosis, 41–2
  measurement of, 117
  normal nature of, 41
  resistance to, 140
  and self-awareness, 106
  as "tension," 52
superstitions, 86
survival, prospects for human,
  157–64
symptom substitution, 144

Temoshok, Lydia and Attkisson,
  Clifford, on anorexia nervosa,
  123
Tobacyk, Jerome, paranormal
  belief scale, 82
Tolstoy, Leo, on "befogging," 80
trance, common everyday, 44
trance logic, 56

Valéry, Paul, 101
Varma, Vijoy, on socio-cultural
  reality of therapy, 140
Vetter, G. B., on superstitious
  belief, 48

Ward, Colleen, on trance
  induction, 135–6
Westman, Alida and Canter,
  Francis, on death anxiety and
  religion, 85
Wiesel, Elie, 104
Wilder, Thornton, 9, 69–70, 146
  on conventions, 77
  on nothingness of life, 24–5
Worsley, Peter, on cargo-cult
  beliefs, 79

Yir-Yiront people, 32

Zilboorg, Gregory, 22–3